# THE BEST MAN

### BY GORE VIDAL

★ **REVISED EDITION**

★

**DRAMATISTS
PLAY SERVICE
INC.**

This version of THE BEST MAN was produced by Jeffrey Richards/Michael B. Rothfeld, Raymond J. Greenwald, Jerry Frankel and Darren Bagert on Broadway at the Virginia Theatre in New York City in September 2000. The associate producers were Francis Finlay, Norma Langworthy and Louise Levathes. It was directed by Ethan McSweeney; the set design was by John Arnone; the lighting design was by Howell Binkley; the sound design and original music were by David Van Tieghem; the costume design was by Theoni V. Aldredge; the hair design was by Bobby H. Grayson; technical supervision was by Neil A. Mazzella; the general manager was Albert Poland; and the production stage manager was Jane Grey. The cast was as follows:

SECRETARY WILLIAM RUSSELL .................... Spalding Gray
ALICE RUSSELL ........................................... Michael Learned
DICK JENSEN ...................................................... Mark Blum
CATHERINE ...................................................... Kate Hampton
SENATOR JOSEPH CANTWELL ......................... Chris Noth
MABEL CANTWELL .................................. Christine Ebersole
DON BLADES ...................................................... Jordan Lage
EX-PRESIDENT ARTHUR HOCKSTADER ..... Charles Durning
MRS. SUE-ELLEN GAMADGE ..................... Elizabeth Ashley
SENATOR CLYDE CARLIN ..................................... Ed Dixon
DELEGATES ........ Joseph Culliton, Joseph Costa, Patricia Hodges
C.J. Wilson, Lee Mark Nelson
DR. ARTINIAN ................................................. Michael Rudko
SHELDON MARCUS .................................. Jonathan Hadary
FIRST REPORTER ......................................... Joseph Culliton
SECOND REPORTER ....................................... Joseph Costa
THIRD REPORTER ...................................... Patricia Hodges
FOURTH REPORTER ............................................ C.J. Wilson
FIFTH REPORTER ...................................... Lee Mark Nelson
ADDITIONAL REPORTERS and HOTEL STAFF .... Kate Hampton
Michael Rudko
NEWS COMMENTATOR ............................. Walter Cronkite

THE BEST MAN was first produced by The Playwrights' Company on Broadway at the Morosco Theatre in New York City in March 1960. The associate producer was Lyn Austin. It was directed by Joseph Anthony; the set and lighting designs were by Jo Mielziner; and the costume design was by Theoni V. Aldredge. The cast was as follows:

| | |
|---|---|
| DICK JENSEN | Karl Weber |
| FIRST REPORTER | Howard Fischer |
| WILLIAM RUSSELL | Melvyn Douglas |
| MIKE | Martin Fried |
| SECOND REPORTER | Tony Bickley |
| THIRD REPORTER | Barbara Berjer |
| FOURTH REPORTER | Tom McDermott |
| ALICE RUSSELL | Leora Dana |
| ASSISTANT TO DICK JENSEN | Ruth Maynard |
| MRS. GAMADGE | Ruth McDevitt |
| ARTHUR HOCKSTADER | Lee Tracy |
| MABEL CANTWELL | Kathleen Maguire |
| BILL BLADES | Joseph Sullivan |
| JOSEPH CANTWELL | Frank Lovejoy |
| SENATOR CARLIN | Gordon B. Clarke |
| DR. ARTINIAN | Hugh Franklin |
| SHELDON MARCUS | Graham Jarvis |
| THREE REPORTERS, DELEGATES, ETC. | John Dorrin, Mitchell Erickson, Ruth Tobin |

# CHARACTERS

SECRETARY WILLIAM RUSSELL
ALICE RUSSELL
DICK JENSEN
CATHERINE
SENATOR JOSEPH CANTWELL
MABEL CANTWELL
DON BLADES
EX-PRESIDENT ARTHUR HOCKSTADER
MRS. SUE-ELLEN GAMADGE
SENATOR CLYDE CARLIN
DR. ARTINIAN
SHELDON MARCUS
FIRST REPORTER
SECOND REPORTER
THIRD REPORTER
FOURTH REPORTER
FIFTH REPORTER

# PLACE

A presidential convention in Philadelphia.

# TIME

Summer 1960.

# SYNOPSIS OF SCENES

## ACT ONE

Scene 1.   A Sheraton Hotel suite.
Scene 2.   Senator Joseph Cantwell's suite. The same evening.

## ACT TWO

Scene 1.   William Russell's suite. The following morning.
Scene 2.   Cantwell suite. A few minutes later.
Scene 3.   Russell suite. A few minutes later.

## ACT THREE

Scene 1.   Cantwell suite. A few minutes later.
Scene 2.   Russell suite. The next morning.

# THE BEST MAN

## ACT ONE

### Scene 1

*A hotel suite in Philadelphia ... perhaps July 1960. From stage right to left: a bedroom with twin beds, a connecting hall and a living room. There is a door from bedroom to hall. At stage right, a door to the bathroom. At stage left, a door to the office part of the suite, from which can be heard telephones ringing and the buzz of talk.*

*Dominating the living room, stage left, is a television set. There is also a bar downstage, a desk upstage and, of course, the usual number of chairs and sofas. The decor is early Conrad Hilton. On the wall, a poster proclaims WILLIAM RUSSELL FOR PRESIDENT. The candidate, according to his portrait, is a strong, youthful-looking man of fifty. There are also various placards around the room, propped against walls and furniture: HUSTLE WITH RUSSELL ... A GREAT GOVERNOR, A GREAT SECRETARY OF STATE, AND THE NEXT PRESIDENT OF THE U.S., and similar political sentiments.*

*Since one hotel suite is apt to look very like another, this same set Could be used For the opposition's suite downstairs, so that when the narrative shifts to the other suite all that would need changing would be specific props: for instance, the placards there would itemize the virtues of Senator Joe Cantwell for president: YOU'LL DO WELL WITH CANTWELL, GO*

*WITH JOE, etc. Fortunately, The Best Man's New York production was designed by John Arnone, using twin turntables which made it possible to have two sets which were shifted with great speed. The Cantwell suite resembled the Russell suite in layout, except that everything was reversed. The Cantwell living room was at right and the bedroom at left. The director made an amiable point in furnishing the Russell bedroom with twin beds and the Cantwell bedroom with a double bed.*

*As the curtain rises, photographers and newsmen set off a great flash of camera bulbs, aimed at William and Alice Russell, who enter from the hall, followed by reporters, photographers, a bellboy and Dick Jensen, Bill Russell's campaign manager.*

*Jensen is in his late forties, intense, devoted, apprehensive by nature. There is a babble of sound: strident questions — "Any statement?" "What about California?" "The labor bill?" "Just one more, Mr. Secretary," "Red China?" "How many delegates you got?" During this, Russell tries to be heard; his wife stands rigidly beside him. Alice Russell is in her early forties. She is a handsome, slender, gray-haired lady of the Old American Establishment, not quite as diffident and shy as she appears.*

JENSEN.  OK, boys! OK. Give him air! One question at a time ...
REPORTER 2.  Mr. Secretary, as of today how many delegates do you have sewed up?
RUSSELL.  *(Lightly.)* When it comes to delegates, we neither sow nor do we reap.
REPORTER 1.  *(Puzzled.)* What was that again, Mr. Secretary?
RUSSELL.  I said ...
JENSEN.  Mr. Russell was making a joke, he means we ...
REPORTER 4.  *(Helpfully.)* He said neither do they sow ...
REPORTER 3.  But what about Ex-President Hockstader? Have you got his endorsement yet?
RUSSELL.  In a word ... no.

REPORTER 2. Do you think you'll get it?

RUSSELL. Ask him. There's a rumor he's in Philadelphia.

REPORTER 5. Yes. He's upstairs. He's going to make a statement tonight. He says it's between you and Senator Cantwell ...

RUSSELL. So we'll just have to wait until tonight.

REPORTER 3. Mrs. Russell, what do *you* think your husband's chances are?

ALICE. *(Uncertainly.)* Well, I ... I don't really know. I mean, we have to wait for the convention, don't we?

REPORTER 4. Mr. Secretary, if there's a deadlock between you and Senator Cantwell, whom do you think will be the dark horse candidate?

RUSSELL. Jack Paar. *(Smiles.)* I'm sorry, but I'm not about to build up a dark horse when I am doing my best to look like the light horse.

REPORTER 2. Sir, what do you think of Governor Merwin's chances?

RUSSELL. John Merwin is a very talented young man. We don't know much about him, of course, but ...

REPORTER 1. *(Quickly.)* Would you consider Governor Merwin as a running mate?

REPORTER 3. Yes.

RUSSELL. I might. He's one of a number of capable men.

REPORTER 5. Mr. Secretary, how did you interpret the Gallup poll this morning?

RUSSELL. I didn't interpret it because I didn't see it.

REPORTER 1. Senator Cantwell's picked up two percent from you since last week ...

JENSEN. *(Overlapping.)* But we're still leading by nine percent in the country with ...

RUSSELL. But you *can* say I don't believe in polls ...

JENSEN. *(Nervously.)* What the Secretary means is ...

RUSSELL. *(Firmly.)* I don't believe in polls. Accurate or not. And if I may bore you with one of my little sermons: Life is not a popularity contest; neither is politics. The important thing for any government is educating the people about issues, *not* following the ups and downs of popular opinion.

REPORTER 3. *(In for the kill.)* Does that mean you don't respect popular opinion? Do you think a president ought to ignore what the people want?

RUSSELL. *(Serenely.)* If the people want the wrong thing, if the people don't understand an issue, if they've been misled by the press *(Politely.)* — by *some* of the press — then I think a president should ignore their opinion and try to convince them that his way is the right way.

REPORTER 1. Do you think the people mistrust intellectuals in politics?

RUSSELL. *(Smiles.)* I'm glad you asked that question. Bertrand Russell seems to think so. He once wrote that the people in a democracy tend to think they have less to fear from a stupid man than from an intelligent one.

REPORTER 4. *(Lost.)* Bertrand...?

RUSSELL. Bertrand Russell.

REPORTER 4. *(Slow, false dawning.)* Oh, the same name ...

RUSSELL. *(Amused.)* Yes. But no relative, unfortunately.

REPORTER 3. *(The taste of blood.)* Wasn't Bertrand Russell *fired* from City College of New York?

RUSSELL. *(Sadly.)* Yes, he was fired. But only for moral turpitude ... *not* for incompetence as a philosopher.

REPORTER 1. What image do you feel Senator Cantwell is projecting at the moment?

RUSSELL. Image? He's behaving himself, if that's what you mean.

REPORTER 1. *(Solemnly.)* But hasn't his *basic* image changed in the last year?

RUSSELL. I'm afraid I don't know much about images. That's a word from advertising where you don't sell the product, you sell the image of the product. And sometimes the image is a fake.

REPORTER 3. *(Slyly.)* But after all, your own image ...

RUSSELL. Is a poor thing but mine own. Paint me as I am, warts and all!

REPORTER 4. What?

RUSSELL. Oliver Cromwell. *(Jensen starts rounding up the press.)*

JENSEN. OK, fellows, we'll have a statement for you in about an hour. Headquarters are through there. The mimeograph machine has been repaired and ...

RUSSELL. And wisdom flows by the yard. *(Jensen herds the*

*reporters off L. All except Reporter 3. She has followed Alice into the bedroom. Russell says goodbye to the reporters at the door.)*
REPORTER 1. *(Urgently.)* Mr. Secretary ... *(A flood of last-minute questions and photographers shouting, "Just one more.")*
RUSSELL. *(Apologetically.)* I have a feeling Dick Jensen would like the candidate to stop talking. I'll see you all later, after the delegations. Until then, as Senator Cantwell would say, may the best man win! *(The reporters and Jensen are gone. Russell is relieved until he hears the cold-edged voice, Reporter 3 in the bedroom.)*
REPORTER 3. How do you like Philadelphia, Mrs. Russell?
ALICE. Well, I just got here ... I used to visit here as a girl. *(Russell comes to the rescue. He propels Reporter 3 to the door U.C.)*
RUSSELL. Please, *please.* Wait till we unpack.
REPORTER 3. Do you drink the tap water?
RUSSELL. I have no intention of losing Pennsylvania by admitting that I boil the local water. *(Reporter 3 departs with an unamused grimace. Russell shudders. Jensen returns.)*
JENSEN. *(Groans.)* Bertrand Russell at a press conference.
RUSSELL. *(Placating.)* All right, Dick, all right, no more jokes. From now on we project blandness. A candidate should not mean but be. And no matter *what* happens, I shall smile: serenely, fatuously, ineluctably. *(Russell, smiling, marches, waving and beaming into the bedroom. Intoning:)* Floods destroy the Middle West, and the candidate smiles. Half the world is starving, and the candidate smiles. War is declared, and the candidate smiles. Is there anything more indecent than the human face when it smiles? *(Russell looks into a mirror.)* All these predatory teeth, reminding us of our animal descent.
JENSEN. Steady. No mention of Darwin. Evolution is out of bounds. Before the Garden of Eden was the Word. And *stop* looking in the mirror.
RUSSELL. I never pass a mirror I don't look in it. I wonder why? *(Alice has gone to hang a garment bag in the bathroom closet. En route she answers him.)*
ALICE. *(Briskly.)* Vanity. *(Alice returns to her luggage in the bedroom.)*
RUSSELL. *(Thoughtfully.)* I look to remind myself I really exist. One needs constant proofs.

ALICE. I better use the bathroom while I've got a chance.

RUSSELL. *(Genuine concern.)* Alice, *don't* drink the *water! (The telephone in the living room rings.)*

JENSEN. *(Answers it.)* Who? Oh, Mrs. Gamadge, good to hear your voice…! Yes, ma'am. Well, he's got the Texas delegation coming in about twenty minutes, but *(Looks to Russell for guidance — Russell nods.)* if you come over right now … Oh, good, you're in the hotel … fine. We'll see you then. *(Puts down receiver.)* Our national committee woman.

RUSSELL. The only known link between the N.A.A.C.P. and the Ku Klux Klan. How does she do it? How? How? *(Russell is studying the carpet as he paces oddly D.)*

JENSEN. *(Curiously.)* Bill … may I ask a very personal question?

RUSSELL. Personal? There is no other kind between us …

JENSEN. What the hell are you doing when you start that hop-scotch thing up and down the floor?

RUSSELL. As we say at press conferences, I'm glad you asked that question. I am … oh, damn! *(He steps back suddenly.)* The ancient Romans used to examine the entrails of animals in order to learn the future. I am told on very good authority that my rival, Senator Cantwell, goes to an astrologist in Kalorama Road, Washington, for guidance. I, lacking all superstition, study the future in multiples of threes. Put simply — and we are nothing if not experts at putting things simply, are we? — I find a carpet with workable pattern. This one's perfect. Now if I step on a leaf — see? — before I have completed three full steps *between* leaves, I will *not* get what I want. If, however, I can take three paces *without* touching that leaf, I will get what I want. I may say, I never cheat. *(Scowls.)* Hell! However, I can on occasion go for the best two out of three. I also make bets with myself. For instance, if the man I'm talking to does not answer me within the count of three, I get what I want. *(He finishes his walk just short of where Jensen is seated.)* Ah, victory! I hope I've answered your question lucidly?

JENSEN. Yes, you have. But let's keep it *our* secret. *(A female aide enters from L. with a stack of newspapers.)*

CATHERINE. Mr. Secretary? *(Russell looks up.)* Sorry to interrupt.

RUSSELL. It's all right, Catherine.

CATHERINE. Here are your newspapers.

RUSSELL. Thanks.

JENSEN. My own vice is the daily horoscope. *(Aide goes.)* So what did you win?

RUSSELL. The nomination. And on the first ballot, too! *(He sits on D. sofa.)* My God, I'm keyed up! I feel like I'm going to jump out of my skin. I can't sit still … *(Jensen crosses to him.)*

JENSEN. Well, you won't do much sitting still between now and Wednesday. Here's today's schedule. Most of the delegations will come to us. *(Shows Russell a piece of paper.)* See? It's a tight schedule, starting with Texas at eleven-fifteen, then …

RUSSELL. *(Unable to attend.)* We're getting so close … so close! And what's going to happen?

JENSEN. You! We've got the delegates. It's yours on the first ballot. *If* you get Ex-President Hockstader's endorsement. *(The door buzzer in the connecting hall sounds. There is a noise of voices in the outside corridor.)*

RUSSELL and JENSEN. *(In unison.)* Mrs. Gamadge! *(Jensen crosses to the hall door and opens it. Mrs. Gamadge sails into view, surrounded by newsmen and photographers. She is serene in the knowledge that she is the Voice of the American Woman, by default. Her manner is an odd mixture of coziness and steeliness.)*

MRS. GAMADGE. *(Beams.)* Mr. Secretary … *(Mrs. Gamadge seizes Russell for a picture. They pose, her left arm around him, her right arm raised in salute. Then Jensen ushers out the press.)*

RUSSELL. *(Sudden energy.)* Mrs. Gamadge, it's wonderful to see you! Come on in. Sit down. Have a drink. You know Dick Jensen, don't you? My campaign manager. *(Mrs. Gamadge shakes Jensen's hand as she crosses to the sofa.)*

MRS. GAMADGE. Such a lovely hotel for a convention. I always say the hotel you're at makes all the difference at a convention. Does Mrs. Russell like your suite?

RUSSELL. Practically a home away from home.

MRS. GAMADGE. *(Narrowly.)* She *is* here with you, isn't she? *(Russell pulls out a chair for her.)*

RUSSELL. Yes. This is the good chair.

MRS. GAMADGE. I'll sit *here,* thank you. *(Mrs. Gamadge unfurls on the sofa.)*

JENSEN. I must say, I'm glad to meet you at last, Mrs. Gamadge.

MRS. GAMADGE. And I'm glad to get a chance to see you, Mr. Jensen. I love eggheads in politics.

JENSEN. *(Taken aback.)* Oh, well …

RUSSELL. *(Quickly.)* What can I get you to drink?

MRS. GAMADGE. I don't drink, Mr. Secretary. A Coke or a glass of soda, maybe. Anything. *(Turns to Jensen. Sweetly:)* Professors like you give such a tone to these conventions. No, I really mean it. Of course a lot of the women don't like them but I do. Though of course I didn't like the New Deal. *(Russell gives her a glass.)*

RUSSELL. Here's your soda … *(She takes it with a nice smile.)*

MRS. GAMADGE. A great many of the women are suspicious of you professors, Mr. Jensen … You don't mind my speaking like this?

JENSEN. Certainly not, Mrs. Gamadge. After all, talking to you is like … well, like talking to the average American housewife. *(Jensen is aware Mrs. Gamadge has frozen on "average." He stammers:)* I mean *you're* not average but you speak for them …

MRS. GAMADGE. Very nicely put, Mr. Jensen. *(To Russell.)* I don't know why everyone says he's so conceited.

RUSSELL. Dick? Stuck up? Why, he's the spirit of humility … an old shoe, in fact! As for being intellectual, he can hardly get through the Greek Anthology without a trot.

MRS. GAMADGE. *(Nods.)* Yes. *(To business.)* You see, the women like a regular kind of man, like General Eisenhower. Now he really appeals to the women. That nice smile. He has such a way with him … he inspires confidence because he doesn't seem like anything but *just folks.* You could imagine him washing up after dinner, listening to his wife's view on important matters.

RUSSELL. *(Quietly.)* Yes, indeed you can.

MRS. GAMADGE. Nothing pushy or aggressive or all those things we women don't like in our men. He's just grand! Now, Mr. Secretary, there is no doubt in anybody's mind you are going to get the nomination on the first ballot.

RUSSELL. There is doubt in *my* mind …

MRS. GAMADGE. *(No time for diversion.)* Yes … yes … yes … now let's face facts a minute. You *don't* mind if I talk turkey?

RUSSELL. No. By all means … turkey.

MRS. GAMADGE. You are not the ideal candidate for the

women. You know that, I suppose.

RUSSELL. Well, what ... what women do you have in mind?

MRS. GAMADGE. *(Coldly.)* The women don't like your trying to be funny all the time.

RUSSELL. Wasn't Abraham Lincoln something of a humorist?

MRS. GAMADGE. The women were not voting in 1860. But they are very suspicious of a man who doesn't take things seriously, so just don't try to be smart-aleck and talk over their heads. I hope you don't mind my talking like this but there isn't much time.

RUSSELL. I am certainly grateful for your ... candor.

MRS. GAMADGE. Now we want to see more of your wife. A lot more.

RUSSELL. She was sick, you know, during the primaries ...

MRS. GAMADGE. And your two fine sons. They're very attractive and that was a nice spread of them in *Life,* at the barbecue. Very, very nice. We'll want more of that. But most important, your wife should be at your side at all times. *(Mrs. Gamadge rises and hands the empty glass to Jensen.)* She must *seem* to be advising you. The women must feel that there is a woman behind you *(Mrs. Gamadge has maneuvered herself into position behind Russell's chair.)* as there has been a woman behind every great man since the world began! *(Russell, aware of Mrs. Gamadge's presence, rises and crosses to Jensen at L.)*

RUSSELL. Alice plans to campaign with me, if ...

MRS. GAMADGE. She's a tremendous asset. I don't need to tell you. The women like the way she doesn't wear makeup and looks like a lady, and seems shy ...

RUSSELL. She is shy.

MRS. GAMADGE. She doesn't make the women feel jealous. And that's good. Keep her with you, Mr. Secretary, at all times. It did Adlai Stevenson great harm, not having a wife, and trying to be funny all the time, too. Great harm. Now I want to ask you a blunt question: What truth is there in the rumor that there has been ... marital discord between you and Mrs. Russell?

RUSSELL. *(Evenly.)* Mrs. Gamadge, my wife is here in Philadelphia. If I am nominated, she will do everything possible to be a helpful candidate's wife ...

MRS. GAMADGE. Could I see her?

RUSSELL. Of course. *(Crosses to bedroom door.)* Alice ... come on out and meet Mrs. Gamadge. *(Alice appears with a toothbrush in her mouth and signals to Russell to wait while she finishes.)*

MRS. GAMADGE. *(To Jensen.)* Now Mabel Cantwell is *such* a nice woman. Really one of the girls. You feel like you've known her all your life. Last time I was in Washington, Mabel gave this lovely dessert luncheon for me with four tables of canasta. *(Somewhat nervously, Alice enters and starts to cross to Mrs. Gamadge, who to Alice's alarm, starts backing away with a speculative look, taking in everything.)*

ALICE. How very nice to see you ...

MRS. GAMADGE. *(Slowly, deliberately.)* You ... couldn't ... look ... better! I mean it! I like the whole thing ... especially the naturally gray hair, that is *such* an important point with the women. Of course Mabel Cantwell dyes her hair, but she gets away with it because she does such a bad job the women feel sorry for her. *(A female aide, Catherine, enters from L. She gives Jensen a note and goes. Jensen shows the note to Russell. Mrs. Gamadge observes this by play.)* Oh, I know you have a million things to do! Anyway, I, just want you to know that I'm for you, Mr. Secretary, and I'm sure you and Mrs. Russell are a winning team. *(To Alice, cozily.)* When you're the First Lady just remember this: Don't do too much ... like Mrs. Roosevelt. The women didn't like that. On the other hand, don't do too little ... like Mrs. Eisenhower. The women don't like that either. All in all, Grace Coolidge was really the best, bless her heart. My husband had such a crush on her ...

JENSEN. How is Mr. Gamadge? *(Russell signals belatedly but the gaffe has been made.)*

MRS. GAMADGE. *(Quietly.)* Mr. Gamadge passed on in 1956. He was stricken during the New Hampshire primaries.

JENSEN. Oh, I didn't know that. I'm sorry ...

MRS. GAMADGE. So am I. He was a fine man, though he didn't like politics. He suffered his terminal thrombosis while I was in Wisconsin, that same year. *(Hearty handclasp.)* Bill, *go to it!* The women are in your corner!

RUSSELL. You don't know how much that means to me ... Sue-Ellen.

MRS. GAMADGE. *(To Alice, warmly.)* Us girls will have a get-together real soon. And that's a promise.

ALICE. I do hope so, Mrs. Gamadge.

MRS. GAMADGE. *(At the door, the knife.)* Oh, by the way! A little bird tells me Joe Cantwell has a surprise for you.

RUSSELL. A surprise?

MRS. GAMADGE. Uh-huh. He's going to smear you with something ... so they say.

RUSSELL. *(Startled.)* Smear me?

MRS. GAMADGE. *(Gaily.)* But here I am telling you what you already know. I'm sure you can handle it. Bye, Bill. Bye, Dick! *(In a burst of sound from the newsmen in the corridor, Mrs. Gamadge goes.)*

ALICE. Smear you, Bill? With what?

RUSSELL. *(Frowns.)* I don't know. *(Jensen waves note.)*

JENSEN. Well, Alice, word has come from on high. We're about to have a visit from our distinguished ex-president.

ALICE. I must say he's one of the ones I like ... except when he tells those long stories.

RUSSELL. Which will it be? The kiss ... or the knife.

JENSEN. How can you miss? Like the rest of us he loves a winner.

ALICE. And he does like *you*, Bill.

RUSSELL. I don't know. He's a funny old bird. *(Catherine appears in doorway, L.)*

JENSEN. Yes?

CATHERINE. The "Volunteer Women for Russell" are on the mezzanine. They want to know if they can see Mrs. Russell.

RUSSELL. Are you up to it?

ALICE. Of course I am. Tell them I'll join them in a few minutes. *(Alice goes into the bedroom to get ready. The aide gives several sheets to Jensen.)*

CATHERINE. Copies of the Secretary's speech for tonight.

JENSEN. I'll check them now. *(Aide goes, L.)*

RUSSELL. *(Indicates speech.)* You might let me look at it, too. I'd like to know what I'm saying.

JENSEN. Come off it, your speech writers ... *(Russell takes the speech and glances through it.)*

RUSSELL. ... are the best money can buy. They have written speeches for Eisenhower, Truman, Dewey, Hockstader, Roosevelt, Hoover and Harold Stassen. Which proves they are men of overpowering conviction.

JENSEN. Do you want to write four speeches a day on top of everything else?

RUSSELL. Of course I want to. But I can't. There isn't time. But it's a shameful business, speech by committee ...

JENSEN. Not to mention *president* by committee. *(Russell hands back the speech.)*

RUSSELL. Please tell the writers *again* that the word "alternative" is always singular. There is only *one* alternative per situation.

JENSEN. I will denounce them as anti-semanticists ... *(Jensen goes off L. Russell, thoughtfully, goes to the desk.)*

RUSSELL. Only one alternative per situation ... unfortunately. That's grammar.

ALICE. *(Dryly.)* And marriage ... Oh, I left my handbag ... *(Alice goes into bedroom, Russell follows.)*

RUSSELL. I'm sorry we're ... in such close quarters.

ALICE. I don't mind. If you don't.

RUSSELL. Odd, after all these years apart. Separate rooms, separate lives.

ALICE. *(Smiles.)* As someone sooner or later says: Politics make strange bedfellows

RUSSELL. Yes.

ALICE. Certainly there's nothing stranger than the two of us in the same room.

RUSSELL. I don't suppose I'm the first candidate to be in this situation.

ALICE. Bill ... don't apologize. I said I'd do what I could to help. And I will. Besides, if I were to ask for a divorce now, you couldn't be president could you?

RUSSELL. I wouldn't count on that.

ALICE. It would be awfully difficult, and it's considered bad form to get rid of the old wife. You know, I really want you to be President.

RUSSELL. Why?

ALICE. I don't know. Perhaps I'm unexpectedly ambitious. Perhaps I want to be First Lady. Or perhaps I look forward to seeing you occasionally. *(Quickly.)* Don't look alarmed! Only in line of duty. You know, an unexpected meeting in the East Room, an ambiguous encounter in the Lincoln Bedroom ...

RUSSELL. *(Amused.)* Alice ...

ALICE. Yesterday, a woman from the press wanted to know what changes I would make when we moved into the White House. I said nothing of a *structural* nature would be changed ... Will it?

RUSSELL. *(Awkwardly.)* You know ... I *do* like the idea of the two of us back together again.

ALICE. *(Suddenly sharp.)* Bill, I am not a delegation from the Legion of Decency. You don't have to charm me. *(Alice starts unpacking, Russell follows suit.)*

RUSSELL. I wasn't trying to. I mean it. I know it's tough ...

ALICE. Tough? Only for you. You're the one who has a problem. How to get girls into the White House. Or will you have a special place on K Street where the president, in disguise of course, can meet new ... people.

RUSSELL. *(From the bathroom.)* Why do you say things like that?

ALICE. Obviously because I'm frustrated. Isn't that the usual excuse women give? And isn't that the usual reason?

RUSSELL. When the desire to make love to someone goes, it goes and nothing on earth can bring it back. Between us, it went.

ALICE. For you.

RUSSELL. I suppose what I wanted in marriage was a friend.

ALICE. And instead you got a very conventional girl who wanted a husband, who wanted ... No. I will *not* put that record on again. I don't know why, but we never manage to say anything new when we get onto the subject of my inadequacy and your ... what shall we call it this time? Athleticism? Since according to the ground rules of our marriage we may call it anything except plain old-fashioned promiscuity.

RUSSELL. Look, if you'd rather not be with me, and have to go through with this ... this gloomy farce, then don't. Quit! Right now. *(Russell scowls and goes into the bathroom with his shaving gear; as he returns he is drawn to the bathroom door mirror.)*

ALICE. Quit? Certainly not. I like circuses. Besides, I'm good for you, isn't that what Dr. Artinian said? After your breakdown? You are the link, he said, between father and sons, between William Russell and the world.

RUSSELL. Dr. Artinian was right.

ALICE. But I wonder what I would have done that summer at Watch Hill, when we first met at the club, if someone had said: "The handsome young man you've just fallen in love with will always need you ... *as a link.*" I think if I had known then what I know now I would have slashed my wrists in front of the buffet table and beautifully bled to death between the chicken salad and the Lobster Newburg.

RUSSELL. *(Smiles.)* Luckily, you are not given to melodrama.

ALICE. Not yet anyway. But you are very nearly a great man and I suppose I can endure anything because of that. Even so, I must insist on my one condition: There is going to be no house on K Street, and no girls in the White House. That is the treaty of suite 674 agreed to this thirty-first day of July, nineteen hundred and sixty, in the city of Philadelphia.

RUSSELL. Agreed. Thank you.

ALICE. So here we are.

RUSSELL. Somewhat past our youth ... and friends?

ALICE. It would be nice if we were, wouldn't it? I really think you'll make a good president.

RUSSELL. But what happens to the treaty if I lose?

ALICE. We go our separate ways, which is what you want. Do I look all right for the "Volunteer Women for Russell"?

RUSSELL. You do.

ALICE. *(Dryly.)* I ought to. I am a founding member of that considerable body. *(Art Hockstader, a former president, in his late seventies but alert despite his years, enters from the bathroom door at R. Hockstader's accent is rural American.)*

HOCKSTADER. Hi, honey ... *(Alice is startled.)*

ALICE. Oh! Mr. President!

HOCKSTADER. You look mighty pretty, Miss Alice ... as usual!

RUSSELL. *(Joining them.)* Mr. President!

HOCKSTADER. Just plain Art Hockstader to you ...

ALICE. Where did you come from?

HOCKSTADER. *(Indicates R.)* Through the privy. There's a door into the next suite. I sneaked through.

ALICE. You look wonderful, after your operation!

HOCKSTADER. Ought to. Nothin' but a hernia from bouncin' my grandson too hard.

RUSSELL. What can I get you to drink? No, no, don't tell me ... bourbon and branch water. *(Russell goes to the living-room bar.)*

HOCKSTADER. With which I shall strike a blow for liberty. *(To the departing Alice.)* Don't let anyone know I'm here. *(Alice nods and goes.)* Well, son, how do you like politics?

RUSSELL. I like it so much I'm beginning to worry.

HOCKSTADER. Awful, ain't it? Worse than gamblin', I sometimes think. Me, I was hooked when I was no more than this high *(Indicates a child.)*, and a certain fourflusher named William Jennings Bryan came to town. His last campaign, I guess ... Well, they shot the works: torch-light parade, picnic, the works! Then finally up there on the back of an old dray, out in a field, this fellow gets up and you never heard such hollerin' from a crowd. Big man he was or so he looked to me, about nine foot tall with hair sweeping over his collar and that square red face of his, and when he spoke I tell you it was like thunder on a summer evenin' and everythin' was still, listenin'. I used to know that speech by heart, it was the famous one. *(Imitates a fustian political voice.)* "You shall not press down upon the brow of labor this crown of thorns."

BOTH. "You shall not crucify mankind upon a cross of gold!"

RUSSELL. Then Bryan lost the election. *(Russell gives Hockstader his drink.)*

HOCKSTADER. So he did, so he did. But it was then and there that a certain farm boy named Art Hockstader said: I am goin' to be a politician and get the folks riled up and eat plenty of barbecue and fried chicken at picnics and have all the pretty girls a-hangin' on my every word.

RUSSELL. *(Carefully.)* Your endorsement, Art, is a very important thing for anybody who wants to be nominated.

HOCKSTADER. I know it is. *(Smiles.)* So, indulge an old duffer! After all, gettin' you fellows to listen to my stories and squirm a bit, waitin' to see who I'm goin' to put my money on, I tell you it's about the only pleasure I got left.

RUSSELL. I'm squirming.

HOCKSTADER. *(Gentle sadism.)* Bill, I have a fatherly feeling about you ...

RUSSELL. And I have ...

HOCKSTADER. *(Continues through him.)* Even though I have

21

certain doubts about you.

RUSSELL. Doubts?

HOCKSTADER. *(Nods.)* I'm kind of responsible for your career. You were *my* Secretary of State, and you were a swell one ... but as you know the people don't give a damn about Secretaries of State. They think the whole foreign thing's a mess anyway and the man who's got to deal with it ... well, I'm afraid the plain folks think the Secretary of State by definition is a foreigner.

RUSSELL. *(Ruefully.)* I know. And if he doesn't like it here he better go back where he came from.

HOCKSTADER. Exactly. Of course you were a fine governor before that. Though Rhode Island is hardly what we call a king-makin' state ... Anyway, it isn't your ability I doubt. Hell, you're ten times as well qualified as I was, and look at me! Possibly one of the greatest statesmen of all time!

RUSSELL. You were pretty good.

HOCKSTADER. I certainly was. *(Dryly.)* Though it's practically our secret right now, as there has been no overpowering popular movement to add me to that rock garden at Mt. Rushmore. But that's not for me to worry about. No, my objection to you, I guess, was prejudice. For one thing you're a Fancy Dan from the East. But I am nothin' if not a realist. The Age of the Great Hicks to which I belong is over. The people trust you rich boys, figurin' since you got a lot of money of your own you won't go stealin' theirs. I'm sure those people who like this Rockefeller are really thinkin' in the back of their minds if they make him president he might decide to pay off the national debt out of his own pocket! If he would, *I'd* vote for him.

RUSSELL. What do you think of Joe Cantwell?

HOCKSTADER. *(Smiles.)* That's a leading question.

RUSSELL. Well, I *am* proposing myself as a leader.

HOCKSTADER. OK, I'll follow. Joe Cantwell is nothin' but ambition. Just plain naked ambition.

RUSSELL. And to get himself elected he will lie ...

HOCKSTADER. *(Nods.)* Yep.

RUSSELL. He will cheat ...

HOCKSTADER. Yep.

RUSSELL. He will destroy the reputations of others ...

HOCKSTADER. Yep.

RUSSELL. Good. So I assume you are endorsing me for the nomination.

HOCKSTADER. Hell, no! Because he's a bastard don't mean he wouldn't be a good candidate. Or even a good president ...

RUSSELL. Joe Cantwell a good...! You're not serious.

HOCKSTADER. Well, he's got a real sense of how to operate.

RUSSELL. To operate? No. To accommodate! If the people are conservative ...

HOCKSTADER. He'll be conservative.

RUSSELL. And if they're radical ...

HOCKSTADER. He'll be radical. Oh, I tell you, son, he is a kind of ring-tailed wonder and don't you underestimate him.

RUSSELL. I don't.

HOCKSTADER. Of course he hasn't got your brains, but then very few of us are as bright as you.

RUSSELL. Now, Art ...

HOCKSTADER. No, I mean it. You are a superior man of the sort we don't get very often in politics. While Joe's just another of the mediocre boys, like me ... only smoother of course. A newer model.

RUSSELL. No, he is *not* like you. He'll do anything to win. And that makes him dangerous.

HOCKSTADER. Now I wouldn't go that far. *(The first turn to the screw.)* At least he knows his own mind.

RUSSELL. And you think I don't know my own mind?

HOCKSTADER. *(Equably.)* Well, son, you got such a good mind that sometimes you're so busy thinkin' how complex everything is important problems don't get solved.

RUSSELL. *(Smiles.)* No, I am not that subtle. I am not that unde-cided. I am not Prince Hamlet.

HOCKSTADER. *(A diversion.)* Hamlet! Lot of fine speeches in that play. Lot of fine speeches in *you,* Bill.

RUSSELL. *(Urgently.)* Art, *don't* support Cantwell!

HOCKSTADER. What makes you think I'm goin' to?

RUSSELL. I mean it. And I am not thinking about myself. I'm thinking about the country.

HOCKSTADER. You got to admit, Joe Cantwell ain't afraid to act.

RUSSELL. Neither am I afraid to act.

23

HOCKSTADER. *(Dreamily.)* Oh? Well, now, I seem to recall how once when you were at a conference with the Russians you were all set to agree to continue nuclear tests, but then when the roof fell in on my administration, I found you had gone and talked yourself up the other side of the street.

RUSSELL. I hesitated only because …

HOCKSTADER. I'll say you hesitated. Now you don't catch Joe Cantwell hesitatin'. No, sir. He's sharp. He's tough.

RUSSELL. He is not tough. He is expedient and that's a very different thing, and I promise you if Joe were president he'd be the greatest appeaser in history.

HOCKSTADER. I would hardly call him an appeaser …

RUSSELL. Suppose the Chinese were to threaten to occupy Taiwan and we were faced with the possibility of a world war, the *last* world war. Now that is the kind of thing you and I understand and I think we could handle it without going to war and without losing Taiwan. But what would Joe do? He would look at the Gallup poll. And what would the Gallup poll tell him? Well, ask the average American, do you want to run the risk of being blown up to save Taiwan? And he'll say, hell, no! Joe would do the popular thing: to hell with Taiwan, and we would be the weaker for it, and that day we're all afraid of would be closer. *(Hockstader finishes his drink and rises.)*

HOCKSTADER. Son, you've been reading too much of that Joe Alsop fellow. Things are never *that* bad! *(Thoughtfully.)* Bill, you know it gets mighty lonely in the White House. Worse for me, I guess, than for you. I'd never lived in a big house with a lot of servants, the way you were brought up. But the worst part is, there's nobody you can believe … that's the awful thing: Everybody's lying to you all day long, Then my wife died … *(Sighs.)* The wonder is that most of us aren't worse than we are. *(Suddenly.)* Bill, do you believe in God?

RUSSELL. *(Startled.)* Do I…? Well, I was confirmed in the Episcopal Church.

HOCKSTADER. Hell, that wasn't what I asked. I'm a Methodist and I'm still askin': Do you believe there's a God and a Day of Judgment and a Hereafter?

RUSSELL. No. I believe in us. In man.

HOCKSTADER. *(Nods.)* I've often pretended I thought there was a God, for political purposes.

RUSSELL. *(Smiles.)* So far I haven't told a lie in this campaign. I've never used the word "God" in a speech.

HOCKSTADER. Well, the world's changed since I was politickin'. In those days you had to pour God over everything, like ketchup. *(He sits on the sofa D.) No,* I don't believe there's a Hereafter. We pass this way just once. And then ... nothing. Bill, I am dying.

RUSSELL. *(Stunned.)* What?

HOCKSTADER. That thing about the hernia was just another lie, I'm afraid. *(Dryly.)* I hope you don't disapprove ... I got the doctors to say the operation was a great success, but it wasn't. I got cancer of the innards and they tell me I may last just long enough to attend the next Inaugural. *(Russell crosses and sits beside him.)*

RUSSELL. Art, I'm...! Look, isn't there ...

HOCKSTADER. There is nothin' they can do, except give me these pills to cut the pain. I tell you, son, I am scared to death. *(Laughs.)* That's a phrase for you: "Scared to death" is exactly right. I don't fancy being nothin', just a pinch of dust. No, sir, I don't like that at all. *(Russell puts his hand on Hockstader's shoulder.)*

RUSSELL. I wish I could say something reassuring, but you wouldn't fall for it anyway. *(Hockstader shrugs away Russell's hand.)*

HOCKSTADER. The only good thing I find is that the rest of you sons of bitches are going to join me. There's some consolation I reckon in that. *(Sighs.)* Oh, I tell you if there is any point to this universe it sure as hell evades me.

RUSSELL. The whole thing's a tragedy. For all of us. But there's hope in this: Every act we make sets off a chain of reaction which never ends. And if we are reasonably ... good, well, there *is* some consolation in that, a kind of immortality.

HOCKSTADER. *(Dryly.)* I suggest you tell yourself that when *you* finally have to face a whole pile of nothin' up ahead. But at the moment I'm alive. And we go into the convention hall day after tomorrow and act like life is all there is ... which, come to think of it, is true. *(Whoops and hollers are heard as Jensen enters from the office at L. Hockstader rises briskly.)*

JENSEN. The Texas Delegation is here. *(Sees Hockstader.)* Oh,

Hello, Mr. ... *(Hockstader motions to Jensen to say nothing. Jensen nods and shuts the door.)*

HOCKSTADER. Bill, don't tell anybody what I told you.

RUSSELL. Of course not.

HOCKSTADER. Meanwhile, I am going to keep you in suspense, until tonight at dinner.

RUSSELL. And then?

HOCKSTADER. I will throw my support like a bridal bouquet to the lucky man. *(Hockstader beams; he starts to cross to the hall; he pauses, then continues to the bedroom.)* Oh, these rumors about you and your lady friends ... won't do you a bit of harm. *But* keep out of trouble. You haven't gone and written any letters like some fellows do?

RUSSELL. *(Smiles.)* No. No letters.

HOCKSTADER. Good boy. She's a nice girl, Alice.

RUSSELL. I think so.

HOCKSTADER. *(Slyly.)* And you never tell a lie, do you? Well, good! Glad to hear it! *(Grimaces with pain.)* Christ, that upper plate of mine pinches! I was going to get a new one but they said it would take a couple of months to make. So I figured I could hold out with what I got.

RUSSELL. Art ... *(There are several whoops and rebel yells from L.)*

HOCKSTADER. You go on in there with those crazy Texans. *(Chuckles.)* I sure wish I was a fly on that wall, listening to you tell the whole *truth* about what you really think of the depletion of the oil resources allowance!

RUSSELL. *(Laughs.)* Get out of here, you old bum ... *(Both men are now in the bedroom. Hockstader smiles, as he crosses to the bathroom door at R.)*

HOCKSTADER. Now is that a respectful way to talk to the end of an era? The last of the Great Hicks as he shuffles off the stage? By way of the privy. *(Hockstader waves as he exits. Russell goes back into the living room. Jensen enters.)*

JENSEN. *(Eagerly.)* Well? What did he say?

RUSSELL. He won't let us know till tonight.

JENSEN. He's going to come out for you. I know it!

RUSSELL. *(Slowly.)* No, he's going to support Joe Cantwell.

JENSEN. *(Startled.)* What! Oh, you're out of your mind. Come

26

on, hurry up, the natives of Texas are getting restless. Now remember on the oil issue …

RUSSELL. I know. I know. Double talk! *(As he follows Jensen off R.)* For those whom we are about to deceive, oh Lord, make us truly compassionate!

## Scene 2

*The Cantwell Suite. A few minutes later. Mabel Cantwell, a blonde pretty woman of forty in a dressing gown, lies on the bed smoking, listening to television and picking out dresses. Around the living room, placards and posters implore us to vote for Senator Joe Cantwell*

COMMENTATOR. *(Voice-over.)* This is Walter Cronkite with the news from Philadelphia. Today, from all across this country, delegates and candidates, party officials, campaign workers, pundits and politicians have descended on this city for the start of the convention. The front-runner, Secretary William Russell and Mrs. Russell flew in this afternoon from their home in Rhode Island

MABEL. *(Perfunctorily.)* Boo!

COMMENTATOR. This morning, Mr. Russell's challenger, Senator Joseph Cantwell, and Mrs. Cantwell arrived.

MABEL. Yea, team! *(Mabel's accent is Southern. She crosses to the living room watching the TV.)*

COMMENTATOR. There they are getting off the train at Thirtieth Street Station *(Mabel is suddenly alert. She studies herself carefully on the screen.)*

MABEL. *(Alarm.)* Oh, my Lord, that hat! *(Mabel crosses to the bar and makes herself a martini.)*

COMMENTATOR. Later, Senator Cantwell rallied his supporters at a press conference held at his hotel. *(On the television screen, a close-up shot of Cantwell.)*

CANTWELL. *(On TV.)* Now don't get me wrong, I have a lot of respect for Bill Russell. But I don't think he's got the people's touch. I think we need a real man of the people for president. Someone like Art Hockstader, who has been an idol of mine all my life.

REPORTER. *(Off camera.)* Senator, Senator ... What about tax reform?

CANTWELL. *(On TV.)* I favor tax reform. I think by cutting down government spending we can eventually eliminate the income tax entirely. *(Mabel kisses the TV and crosses back to the bedroom.)*

REPORTER. *(Off camera.)* So you feel we can increase military spending while eliminating the income tax?

CANTWELL. *(On TV.)* And I think it's a pretty swell thing that in a country like this someone like me from a poor family can come here before you, speaking for the real people of America. All I can say is that come Wednesday, I only hope that the best man wins! May the best man win.

MABEL. *(Overlapping.)* ... the best man win. *(There is a noise of reporters as the hall door opens. Mabel rushes into the bedroom, shutting the door behind her. Don Blades ushers the smiling Joe Cantwell into the living room. Cantwell is in his forties. His manner is warm, plausible. Though under great tension, he suggests ease. He has a tendency not to listen when preoccupied. He poses for one more photograph, arms victoriously raised. Then Blades gets the reporters out. Cantwell and Blades are drawn into watching the TV which is reporting Gallup poll statistics.)*

BLADES. That went well, Joe. *(Turns off TV.)* You better rest before dinner.

CANTWELL. About Hockstader, what did he say when you saw him? What *exactly* did he say?

BLADES. *(For the hundredth time.)* He said he hadn't made up his mind, but he would by tonight.

CANTWELL. Mabel, honey! Come on out. It's just Don Blades and me. *(Mabel appears. She throws herself on Cantwell. They embrace warmly. Laughing.)* Hey, come on! You better get dressed. We got to go down to dinner in *(Looks at watch.)* thirty minutes.

MABEL. I'll be ready ... don't you worry, baby. Fix yourself a drink, Don. *(Blades is at the bar upstage.)*

BLADES. Can I get you anything, Mabel?

MABEL. Oh, no, I don't think so. I don't ... well, maybe just the teeniest martini, to settle my stomach. *(Concern.)* Oh, Joe, you look so tired.

CANTWELL. *(Automatically.)* Never felt better. *(Cantwell picks, up a newspaper and reads, frowning.)*

MABEL. Well, I finally got through the women's tea and I've been here watching the TV. We got awful nice coverage, Joe ... though that new hat of mine is clearly a mistake. It looks like I have no chin, but even with no chin I certainly look better than Alice Russell. My God, she is a chilly-looking woman, just like an English teacher I had back at State College, the spittin' image ... from Boston she was and always wore her hair in this bun with no makeup and of course thought she was the cat's meow ... *(Blades gives her a drink.)*

BLADES. Here you go, Mabel.

MABEL. Thank you, Don.

CANTWELL. Hey, Don, that joke of yours looks pretty good.

BLADES. Oh? Which one was that?

CANTWELL. *(Reads.)* "At his press conference yesterday, Senator Cantwell quipped: 'Bill Russell has more solutions than there are problems.'" *(Mabel tastes the martini. She sighs.)*

MABEL. *(To Cantwell.)* All the papers say Hockstader's going to come out for Bill Russell, heaven knows why, with your record in the Senate ...

CANTWELL. *(Shuts his eyes.)* I am tired. *(Then he rises, abruptly. He turns to Blades.)* I got to see Hockstader. Right now. Before that dinner.

BLADES. What are you going to tell him?

CANTWELL. Everything. The works. Maybe he won't come out for me afterwards but he'll sure drop Bill Russell.

BLADES. *(Rises.)* OK. You're the boss.

CANTWELL. Go on up there. He's on the seventh floor. Tell him I've *got* to see him before dinner which is in *(Looks at watch.)* twenty-seven minutes.

BLADES. Aye, aye, my captain. *(Cantwell is on his feet. He turns irritably to Mabel.)*

CANTWELL. Mabel, come on, get dressed!

MABEL. I'll be ready, Joe, stop worryin' ... don't get all het up. *(She embraces him.)* Why is big Poppa Bear so mean to poor little

29

Mama Bear?

CANTWELL. Baby, I'm sorry. *(He goes into their private baby talk.)* Poppa Bear is never mean to his Mama Bear, never ever. *(His own voice.)* But, honey, you've *got* to get dressed!

MABEL. OK, I will ... I will. Joe, when are you going to spring that ... that stuff about Bill Russell?

CANTWELL. Tomorrow.

MABEL. The *whole* thing?

CANTWELL. Pow! *(He crosses into the bedroom, searching in his suitcase and then in the vanity for his razor.)*

MABEL. *(Rapturously.)* And then we are on our way to 1600 Pennsylvania Avenue! *(She crosses into the bedroom.)* Oh, my, it's thrilling, isn't it? Seems just like yesterday we were skimpin along hardly able to pay the bills to have Gladys' teeth straightened, and now just look at us! Poppa Bear and Mama Bear and the baby bears all in the White House!

CANTWELL. Where's my electric razor?

MABEL. I'll get it! *(She goes quickly into the bathroom.)* I'll just start putting on my clothes and ... *(She finds the razor and gives it to him.)*

CANTWELL. Where's that last Gallup poll?

MABEL. I think Don Blades got it. Anyway, you're two percent higher than last week with twelve percent undecided. Merwin gained one percent and Russell's lost two percent.

CANTWELL. And Red China?

MABEL. *(Promptly.)* Forty-seven percent against recognition. Twenty-three percent in favor. Thirty percent don't know. I'm wearing the green organza tonight, the one from Neiman Marcus, Donald Brooks sent me. I think it looks real summery and nice ...

CANTWELL. *(Frowns.)* That's not enough in favor. Russell's a fool making an issue out of China this soon ... *(Mabel removes her dressing gown and starts to get into her dress offstage.)*

MABEL. I had my hair done this morning by the man in the hotel; he's very nice but terribly swishy. Anyway he didn't get the curls too tight ... At least I don't think so. He said Alice Russell had her hair done, too. *(Unnoticed by Mabel, Cantwell turns on the electric razor and reads a newspaper.)* He said she refuses to entertain the thought of using so much as a rinse. Well, bully for her!

She looks easily ten years older than she is. *(Frowns.)* Joe, do you think I've gained weight? Around the hips? Honey, you listenin' to me? *(Realizing he is preoccupied, Mabel, pouting, crosses and sits on the bed.)* No, I guess you're not ... You never listen to poor Mama Bear anymore. *(Pause.)* Joe? Have you ever been unfaithful to me?

CANTWELL. *(Turns off razor.)* No. Did you see Walter Lippmann this morning. Listen to what that guy says: "The country's affairs will be in good hands should William Russell be our next president." I don't know why I don't appeal to those would-be intellectuals. My image just doesn't project to them like his does. *(Mabel presents herself D. He notices Mabel at last, slaps the paper down.)* Well, look at you! Just good enough to eat. *(He starts to nuzzle her in a bearish way.)* Mmm — mm —

MABEL. *(Happily nuzzled.)* Now what are you doing to me? Don't muss my hair! Now come on! Stop it! And zip me up! *(She turns around. As Joe zips her dress, she returns to her theme.)* Joe, are you sure you haven't been unfaithful to me maybe just one little time? On one of those junkets? Like that awful one to Paris you took, where the senators got drunk and Clarence Wetlaw contracted a social disease and Helen Wetlaw was fit to be tied?

CANTWELL. Mabel, honey, there's nobody else. And even if there was, how would I have the time? I operate on a tight schedule. *(Kisses her briefly.)* You know that. *(Blades enters from corridor door.)*

BLADES. Joe, I talked to Hockstader.

CANTWELL. Well?

BLADES. He'll be right down.

CANTWELL. And?

BLADES. Not a clue.

CANTWELL. OK. Get me that file on Russell. *(To Mabel, indicating bedroom.)* Honey, you go in there ... fix your face or something. The president's on his way down.

MABEL. Joe ... play it cool, like the kids say now.

CANTWELL. I will. *(Mabel nods and crosses to the bathroom. Cantwell crosses to the living room. Blades gives him a manila folder.)*

BLADES. This ought to do the trick.

CANTWELL. I'll say it will. *(Turns the pages.)* Oh, cute. Very cute. How's the New York delegation?

BLADES. Still split down the middle.

CANTWELL. Well, they won't be split after this. *(A sound of excited voices from corridor.)*

BLADES. Here he comes. Are you ready? *(Cantwell nods; he takes a position at stage R.)*

CANTWELL. All set. *(Warningly.)* Don: Remember … flatter him! *(Blades nods, opens the door. Hockstader, in evening dress, pushes his way through a mob of newsmen.)* Mr. President! *(Cantwell beams and crosses to Hockstader as Blades shuts out the press.)*

HOCKSTADER. Hello, Blades … Hi, Joe! *(Hockstader indicates the corridor door.)* Well, this ought to start some rumors. *(Cantwell is now shaking his hand warmly.)*

CANTWELL. Gosh, I'm sorry, sir. We should've arranged for you to come in the back way.

HOCKSTADER. Oh, that's all right. We're gettin' near that time anyway. *(Taps coat pocket.)* Got my speech right here. My teeth are in and I'm rarin' to go. *(Indicates Cantwell.)* What about you? Where's your party suit?

CANTWELL. *(Seriously.)* I have it all timed. It takes me exactly three minutes to get into a tux. Two minutes for an ordinary business suit, and that's including vest.

HOCKSTADER. Well, ain't you a ring-tailed wonder? *(Crosses to bar.)* You don't mind if I strike myself a blow for liberty?

CANTWELL. Let me … please … *(Gestures to Blades to help.)* Don!

HOCKSTADER. *(Fixes his own drink.)* That's all night. I know Joe doesn't have the habit. People who don't drink never realize how thirsty we old bucks get long 'round sundown. *(Turns thoughtfully to Cantwell.)* No, sir, you don't drink, you don't smoke, you don't philander; fact, you are about the purest young man I have ever known in public life.

CANTWELL. I try to be.

HOCKSTADER. Well, I am a great admirer of virtue, though a somewhat flawed vessel of grace myself. *(Hockstader sits on sofa.)*

CANTWELL. Now, Mr. President … you're an ideal to us in the party.

HOCKSTADER. *(Dryly.)* Sure, Joe, sure … Young man, you've done a remarkable job in the Senate. Most of the time.

CANTWELL. *(Quickly.)* *Most* of the time?

32

HOCKSTADER. *(Nods.)* There *have* been moments when I have questioned your methods.

CANTWELL. Well, you have to fight fire with fire, Mr. President.

HOCKSTADER. And the end justifies the means?

CANTWELL. Well, yes, sir. Yes. That is what I believe.

HOCKSTADER. Well, son, I have news for you about both politics and life ... and may I say the two are *exactly* the same thing? There are no ends, Joe, only means.

CANTWELL. Well, I don't like to disagree with you, sir, but that's just sophistry. I mean ...

HOCKSTADER. *(Amused.)* Now! None of them two-bit words on poor old Art Hockstader. I'm just an ignorant country boy. And all I'm saying is that what matters in our profession ... which is really life ... is *how* you do things and how you treat people and what you really feel about 'em, not some ideal goal for society, or for yourself.

CANTWELL. *(His district-attorney voice.)* Then am I to assume, Mr. President, from the statement you have just made, that you are against planning anything?

HOCKSTADER. *(Laughs.)* Oh, here it comes! I know that voice! Senator Cantwell, boy crusader, up there on the TV with these small-time hoodlums cringing before his righteousness.

BLADES. *(To the rescue.)* Now, Mr. President, Joe was *assigned* that subcommittee. He didn't ask for it ... and that's a fact.

HOCKSTADER. Sure. Sure. And he just fell into that big issue: how the United States is secretly governed by the Mafia.

CANTWELL. It happened to be true. Anytime you want to look at my files, Mr. President ...

HOCKSTADER. Last time somebody asked me to look at his files, it was Senator McCarthy.

CANTWELL. *(Grimly.)* I hope, sir, you're not comparing me to him.

HOCKSTADER. No ... no, Joe. You're a much smoother article. After all, you've got an end to which you can justify your means, getting to be president. Poor old McCarthy was just wallowing in headlines ... sufficient to the day were the headlines thereof. No, you're much brighter, much more ruthless.

CANTWELL. I realize some of my methods upset a lot of people, particularly criminals …

BLADES. *(Righteously.)* Mr. President, if we hadn't been tough we would never have cracked the Mafia the way we did. *(Hockstader smiles during this.)*

CANTWELL. What's so funny about that, sir?

HOCKSTADER. Nothing, only you know and I know and everybody knows … except I'm afraid the TV audience … that there never was a Mafia like you said. There was no such thing. You just cooked it up.

CANTWELL. *(Dangerously.)* So we're going to get that number, are we? Well, my figures prove …

HOCKSTADER. *(Sharply.)* You went after a bunch of poor Sicilian bandits on the Lower East Side of New York and pretended they were running all the crime in America. Well, they're not. Of course we have a pretty fair idea who is, but you didn't go after any of them, did you? No, sir, because those big rascals are heavy contributors to political campaigns.

BLADES. *(Beginning.)* Maybe Joe didn't go after all of them, sir …

HOCKSTADER. Just barely scratched the surface …

CANTWELL. But *you* should talk. J. Edgar Hoover considered you the most morally lax president in his entire career …

HOCKSTADER. *(Serenely.)* I reserve my opinion of J. Edgar Hoover for a posthumous memoir or maybe a time capsule to be dug up when he has finally cleansed the republic of undesirables.

CANTWELL. Hoover is a great American!

HOCKSTADER. *(Amused.)* We're all "great Americans," Joe. *(More seriously.)* No, I don't object to your headline-grabbing and crying "wolf" all the time, that's standard stuff in politics, but it disturbs me you take yourself so seriously. It's par for the course trying to fool the people but it's downright dangerous when you start fooling yourself. *(Mabel Cantwell, in the bedroom, has heard voices grow angry. She crosses and listens at the bedroom door.)*

CANTWELL. *(Carefully.)* Mr. President, I take myself seriously. Because I am serious. This is important to me. To all of us. Which is why I don't want any little lectures from you on how to be a statesman. And if you really want to know, I think the record of your administration is one of the heaviest loads our party has to carry. *(Hockstader is on his feet, suddenly furious. Mabel enters.)*

MABEL. Why, Mr. President! What a nice surprise, your dropping in on us like this! *(Hockstader regains his composure.)*

HOCKSTADER. Well, I was invited down here by this young man for a little conference, and here he is, filling my head with sweet nothings.

MABEL. *(Rapturously.)* Joe admires you, I guess, more than any man in public life.

CANTWELL. *(To Mabel.)* Honey, leave us alone. *(Indicates to Blades that he leave, too.)* Don. *(Blades exits R.)*

MABEL. All right, but Joe, you have to get dressed soon.

CANTWELL. OK.

MABEL. You certainly look fine, Mr. President, after your little vacation in the hospital …

HOCKSTADER. Fit as a fiddle. Never felt better. *(Mabel goes into the bedroom. She shuts the door. She listens.)*

CANTWELL. I'm sorry, sir, flying off the handle like that.

HOCKSTADER. *(Smiles.)* That's OK. You just got a case of the old pre-convention jitters … Now I assume you didn't ask me down here to discuss the virtues of J. Edgar Hoover. *(Hockstader crosses to the bar D. He fixes himself another drink.)*

CANTWELL. No, I didn't. *(Awkwardly.)* I know you don't like me …

HOCKSTADER. Now that you mention it, I don't. I never have.

CANTWELL. And I've never liked your kind of politician. But that's neither here nor there. I don't expect you to come out for me tonight …

HOCKSTADER. I should warn you I have often endorsed men I disliked, even mistrusted, because I thought they'd do the job. *(Cantwell has gone to the desk. He picks up the file and crosses back to the coffee table. Hockstader suffers a spasm of pain at the bar. He clutches his stomach. Cantwell does not notice this.)*

CANTWELL. So I have something to show you about your friend William Russell. It's all here in this file. I want you to look at it and … *(Cantwell looks at Hockstader; he realizes something is wrong.)* What's the matter with you?

HOCKSTADER. *(With difficulty.)* Just … had to take one of my pills. *(Takes a pill.)* Pep me up. *(Cantwell nods. He sits. Hockstader looks at him thoughtfully.)* Joe, you believe in God, don't you?

CANTWELL. *(Promptly.)* Yes, I do.

HOCKSTADER. And you believe there's a Hereafter? And a Day of Judgment?

CANTWELL. *(Sincerely.)* I do. If I didn't think there was some meaning to all of this I wouldn't be able to go on. I'm a very religious guy, in a funny way. *(Cantwell spreads the contents of the folder on the coffee table.)*

HOCKSTADER. I'm sure you are. *(Sighs.)* Times like this I wish I was. Dying is no fun, let me tell you. And that's what I'm doing. *(Cantwell has not been listening.)*

CANTWELL. *(Briskly.)* Now it's all here. Psychiatrist reports ... everything. And don't ask *how* I got it. My means might've been ruthless but for once I think you'll agree the end was worth it. *(Hockstader is taken aback at being ignored. He comes D. He indicates the papers contemptuously.)*

HOCKSTADER. What is all this ... crap?

CANTWELL. Several years ago *your* candidate, William Russell, had what is known as a nervous breakdown.

HOCKSTADER. I know that.

CANTWELL. He was raving mad for almost a year.

HOCKSTADER. He was not raving mad. It was exhaustion from overwork ...

CANTWELL. That was the press release. The real story's right here ...

HOCKSTADER. I know the real story.

CANTWELL. Then you know it's political dynamite. A full report on his mental state. How he deserted his wife, how their marriage has always been a phony, a political front ...

HOCKSTADER. I won't begin to speculate on how you got hold of this ...

CANTWELL. And all the big words are there, manic-depressive, paranoid pattern, attempted suicide ...

HOCKSTADER. He never attempted suicide.

CANTWELL. I'm sorry. It says right here that he did. See? *(Points to page.)* There. Suicidal tendencies ...

HOCKSTADER. We've all got suicidal *tendencies*. But he never tried to kill himself.

CANTWELL. But the point is he *could.*

HOCKSTADER. I thought you said he *did* try.

CANTWELL. I did not say he did. I said he could. And then all that combined with playing around with women …

HOCKSTADER. So what?

CANTWELL. I suppose you find promiscuity admirable?

HOCKSTADER. I couldn't care less. I was brought up on a farm and the lesson of the rooster was not entirely lost on me. A lot of men need a lot of women and there are worse faults, let me tell you.

CANTWELL. *(Suspiciously.)* What do you mean by that?

HOCKSTADER. Just that there are rumors about every public man. Why, when I was in the White House they used to say I had paresis, and how I was supposed to be keepin' this colored girl over in Alexandria, silliest damn stories you ever heard but it gave a lot of people a lot of pleasure talkin' about it. You know, when that Kinsey fellow wrote that book about how many men were doin' this and how many men were doin' that, I couldn't help but think how right along with all this peculiar activity there was a hell of a lot of *nothin'* goin on!

CANTWELL. All right, leaving the moral issue out, do you think it a good idea to elect a man president who is mentally unstable?

HOCKSTADER. He is not mentally unstable and you know it.

CANTWELL. *(Inexorably.)* A manic-depressive? Apt to crack up under stress? *(Hockstader gets the point.)*

HOCKSTADER. So that's your little number, is it?

CANTWELL. *(Evenly.)* If Russell doesn't withdraw before Wednesday, I am going to see that every delegate gets a copy of this psychiatric report and I am going to challenge Russell openly. I'm going to ask him if he really feels that a man with his mental record should be President of the United States. Frankly, if I were he, I'd pull out before this *(Indicates papers.)* hits the fan.

HOCKSTADER. Well, you are *not* Russell … to state the obvious. And he might say in rebuttal that after his breakdown he served a right rough period as Secretary of State and did not show the strain in any way.

CANTWELL. One of the psychiatrists reports that this pattern of his is bound to repeat itself. He is bound to have another breakdown.

HOCKSTADER. You and your experts! You know as well as I do those head-doctors will give you about as many different opinions as you want on any subject.

CANTWELL. *(Reasonably.)* I realize that, which is why I am going to propose that he be examined, before Wednesday, by a nonpartisan group of psychiatrists to determine if he is sane.

HOCKSTADER. You know he won't submit to that.

CANTWELL. If he doesn't, that means he has something to hide.

HOCKSTADER. Wow! You sure play rough, don't you?

CANTWELL. I regard this as a public service. *(Urgently.)* Look, I'm not asking you to support me. I don't even *want* your support. But I do want you to think twice before endorsing a man who is known to be psychopathic.

HOCKSTADER. You got it figured, of course, that even to hint that a man's not right in his head will be enough to knock him off? When do you plan to throw this at him?

CANTWELL. Tomorrow.

HOCKSTADER. And of course you've waited for the last minute so he won't have a chance to clear himself before the convention starts. That's right smart.

CANTWELL. *(Not listening.)* We'll have to work out some way for him to withdraw gracefully. I thought maybe he could say … well, nervous exhaustion … doesn't feel up to the rigors of a campaign, something like that.

HOCKSTADER. And if he doesn't quit "gracefully"?

CANTWELL. *(Taps folder.)* This will be circulated. And I will demand he be examined by psychiatrists.

HOCKSTADER. I suppose you realize you are now open to the same kind of treatment.

CANTWELL. I have nothing to hide in my private or public life.

HOCKSTADER. Are you absolutely certain?

CANTWELL. *(Carefully.)* Just … try … anything.

HOCKSTADER. Well, looks like we're gonna have an ugly fight on our hands. Yes, sir, a real ugly fight. So now I am going to let you have it. And when I finish with you, my boy, you will know what it is like to get in the ring with an old-time killer. I am going to have your political scalp and hang it on my belt, along with a lot of others.

CANTWELL. *(Dangerously.)* Don't mix with me, Hockstader.

HOCKSTADER. You can't touch me. But I can send you back to the insurance business. *(He crosses U. to exit, pauses and turns. He removes his speech from his pocket, almost sadly.)* And just think! I was going to endorse *you* for President.

CANTWELL. I don't believe you.

HOCKSTADER. It's not that I mind your bein' a bastard, don't get me wrong there ... It's your bein such a *stupid* bastard I object to. *(Contemptuously, Hockstader tosses the speech at Cantwell's feet. Then he turns and exits to the corridor, flinging the doors open. Flashbulbs go off. As Hockstader disappears into the crowd of newsmen, Cantwell picks up the speech and starts to read.)*

### Scene 3

*The Russell suite. The next afternoon. A delegation is being shown out by Russell and Jensen. They pump hands. Russell placards are waved. At the bar stands Senator Carlin, a ponderous politician of the prairies.*

JENSEN. OK, gentlemen ... we'll see you tomorrow, in the convention hall.

DELEGATE. *(To Russell, warmly.)* Bill, we'll nominate you on the first ballot tomorrow ... and that's a promise ...

RUSSELL. *(Smiles.)* If nominated, I will run. If elected, I will serve. Thanks.

JENSEN. *(To the last delegate.)* We'll be in touch with you ... *(To Russell.)* Well, what do you think?

RUSSELL. Looks all right. Nobody's mentioned mental health yet.

CARLIN. What *did* you fellows think of Hockstader's speech last night? *(Both Russell and Jensen turn, startled.)*

RUSSELL. Senator Carlin! I thought you'd left ...

CARLIN. No. Just stayed to fix myself a snort, if you don't mind. Now about Hockstader's speech last night ...

RUSSELL. Well, I was surprised as anybody.

CARLIN. You thought he was going to endorse you?

JENSEN. *(Quickly.)* We certainly did.

CARLIN. And then the old man just got up and talked plain double talk …

JENSEN. At least he didn't endorse Cantwell. *(Jensen goes off L.)*

CARLIN. No. He didn't endorse *nobody*. For a minute I thought he was going to surprise us and come out for John Merwin, just to be ornery. Now I hear you were with the old man later on last night. What's he up to? My boys think a lot of old Art and they'll go along with him …

RUSSELL. We were having a council of war, I guess you'd call it.

CARLIN. They say Joe's got something on you, something pretty bad.

RUSSELL. Something untrue. And frankly I'm not very worried. I'm a lot more worried about the labor plank in the platform …

CARLIN. *(Exasperated.)* Oh, Christ, Bill! Lay off labor, will you? You got their vote now, so don't go stirring up a lot of snakes. After all, *you're* the liberal candidate …

RUSSELL. What is a liberal, Senator? *(Russell crosses to desk, picks up a dictionary, thumbing pages.)*

CARLIN. *(Groans.)* And I thought Adlai Stevenson was a pain in the neck. A liberal is a … well, you, Bill Russell, are a liberal, that's what a liberal is. You.

RUSSELL. According to the dictionary a liberal is one who "favors changes and reforms tending in the direction of further democracy." Well, I am in favor of further democracy for the unions' rank and file …

CARLIN. Bill, please … I'm just a poor dumb party hack …

RUSSELL. I'm sorry, Senator. The terrible thing about running for president is you become a compulsive talker, forever answering questions no one has asked you.

CARLIN. Well, let me ask *you* a question. Would you consider offering the vice president nomination to Cantwell?

RUSSELL. No.

CARLIN. *(Sourly.)* For a compulsive talker, you sure don't have much to say on that subject. *(Sighs.)* Jeez, I hate an open convention. You can't ever tell what's going to happen!

RUSSELL. *(Smiles.)* They're never that open.

CARLIN. I suppose we better try for a Catholic … that seems to be the big thing this year … for *second* place, that is. *(Jensen returns with newspapers.)* Bill, *don't* make things tough for yourself! You got the nomination now so leave the controversial things alone.

RUSSELL. I can't help it. I am driven by a mad demon, by some imp of the perverse … *(Carlin looks at Russell narrowly. Jensen gives him a warning look.)* That is, I am *compelled* to say what I think.

CARLIN. OK, but try to lay off stuff like Red China, especially when you know Henry Luce is an absolute nut on China and you don't want to lose *Time* and *Life* when they're already behind you in the interests of good government and all that baloney … So keep Henry Luce happy, will you? Once you're president, you can eat with chopsticks for all anybody cares.

RUSSELL. I will be diplomatic.

CARLIN. You know, Cantwell's releasing a statement today. To all the delegates. He says it'll knock you off.

RUSSELL. We're ready for him. He may be the master of the half truth and the insinuation but we've got the facts.

CARLIN. And the *whole* truth?

RUSSELL. *(Lightly.)* No man has the whole truth.

CARLIN. Oh, brother! Good luck, Bill. Let me know if there's anything I can do for you. I'm with you one hundred percent, in spite of your damned dictionary.

RUSSELL. Thank you, Senator. *(Carlin goes. Russell is drawn to the carpet and his game.)* Dick, where's Dr. Artinian?

JENSEN. On his way from the airport.

RUSSELL. And Hockstader?

JENSEN. Talking to delegates … Bill, I've finally got a line on Cantwell. I got some real dirt …

RUSSELL. Of all the stunts, this is the craziest! If you'll excuse my obsessive use of words like "mad" and "crazy."

JENSEN. You could've cut the air with a knife when you made that crack about being "driven by a mad demon" … *(Russell has started his walk across the carpet.)*

RUSSELL. Well, they reelected Eisenhower after a heart attack and an ileitis operation … didn't seem to hurt him.

JENSEN. But there was never any question about his mind or his judgment being affected. *(Russell has completed his walk.)* Well? What's the score?

RUSSELL. *(Smiles.)* I still get it on the first ballot but it was a near miss: I nearly stepped on that leaf, the one by the table ... it's a bitch. *(Indicates newspaper, sits on coffee table.)* What about your daily horoscope?

JENSEN. *(From memory.)* "A.M. Fine for getting apparel in order. P.M. Do not quarrel with loved one." Bill, you may have to pull a Nixon.

RUSSELL. And what does "pull a Nixon" mean?

JENSEN. Go on television. And cry on the nation's shoulder. With *two* cocker spaniels.

RUSSELL. And tell them I'm not crazy? No. I admit it's possible to look directly into a camera and persuade the people I won't steal their money, but I promise you, Dick, you can't look a camera in the face and say "Honest, I'm not crazy — I just had a nervous breakdown like any regular fellow might." No, it won't work.

JENSEN. Why not?

RUSSELL. Because it won't. And even if it did, I couldn't do it. *(Chuckles.)* I might ... laugh. It's too idiotic. *(Alice enters from corridor door, Russell rises and crosses D. L.)* How was the meeting?

ALICE. I made a speech. At least I started to read the one Dick gave me. Then halfway through I gave up and made my own speech, and do you know what? It was terrible! *(Suddenly grave.)* What's happened?

RUSSELL. Dr. Artinian's on his way to Philadelphia. He's going to tell the press that I am not and never was insane.

ALICE. It gets worse and worse, doesn't it?

RUSSELL. Yes, it does. *(Jensen rises, crosses to the desk, picks up schedules and heads to office door.)*

JENSEN. I've got to get back to work. Here. *(He hands schedules to Russell.)* We have Florida in twenty minutes. Then one more go at California.

RUSSELL. Send Dr. Artinian in the second he gets here. *(Jensen nods, exits L.)*

ALICE. Does this mean they could publish everything about us? Our marriage and ... *everything?*

RUSSELL. Yes. *(Alice sits on the coffee table.)*

ALICE. Will they?

RUSSELL. I don't know. I think it's just a bluff right now, to frighten me.

ALICE. It frightens me. I should hate to think of the children reading all that about us. Oh, it is filthy … filthy!

RUSSELL. Do you want me to quit?

ALICE. *(A pause.)* No. *(Russell puts his hand on Alice's; she smiles.)* How very odd!

RUSSELL. What?

ALICE. Do you realize that this is the first time you've touched me when there wasn't a camera or someone in the room? *(There is a tense moment; then he pats her hand briskly and pulls out the schedules.)*

RUSSELL. Well, here's your schedule. Your next appointment is … Oh, my God, I forgot all about this!

ALICE. *(Grimly.)* I haven't. Mabel Cantwell and I face the press together. Can I get out of it?

RUSSELL. No. Better not.

ALICE. Then I'll get ready. We're meeting in her suite. She made the point very tactfully over the phone that *(Alice lapses into deep Mabelese.)* accordin' to protocol the wife of a reignin' Senator out-ranks the wife of a former Secretary of State.

RUSSELL. *(Equally Southern.)* Well, bless my soul! *(Alice goes. Dr. Artinian, a distinguished-looking psychiatrist enters with Jensen from L. Russell crosses to greet him, just as the buzzer from the corridor sounds. Jensen hurries to corridor door.)* Robert, I'm glad you could get away like this …

ARTINIAN. I had to. *(Jensen opens corridor to admit Hockstader, who darts in while Jensen pushes back the press.)*

RUSSELL. Dr. Artinian … President Hockstader.

HOCKSTADER. You Bill's head-doctor?

ARTINIAN. That's right. And I'm a very great admirer of yours, Mr. President.

HOCKSTADER. Well, I'm *not* an admirer of yours. Why don't you people keep your damned files where nobody can get at 'em?

ARTINIAN. We do. Or we thought we did. Apparently some-body from Cantwell's office bribed one of our nurses … they got the entire case history.

RUSSELL. Robert, in one hour Cantwell's releasing that file on me. Now I know this sounds silly, but when he does, I want you to meet the press and tell them I am *not* mentally unstable.

ARTINIAN.  Of course I will. You don't know how guilty I feel about this.

HOCKSTADER.  *(Suddenly.)* He *is* all right, isn't he?

ARTINIAN.  *(Smiles.)* Mr. Russell is one of the sanest men I ever have known.

HOCKSTADER.  Then what's all that stuff about suicide tendencies and manic-mania or whatever you call it?

ARTINIAN.  Just technical phrases which may sound sinister to a layman. He is certainly *not* a manic-depressive. Anyone's psychological profile could be made to sound ... damaging.

RUSSELL.  *(Lightly.)* In the South a candidate for sheriff once got elected by claiming that his opponent's wife had been a thespian. *(Jensen opens the door to the office.)*

JENSEN.  We'll find a room for you here, Doctor. And I'll get somebody to help you with your statement.

ARTINIAN.  Thank you. I also brought the Institute's lawyer with me. By way of making amends, Bill, we're filing suit against Cantwell for theft ...

HOCKSTADER.  *(Pleased.)* That's the ticket. Go to it, Doc.

ARTINIAN.  *(To Russell.)* I'll be ready when you want me.

RUSSELL.  *(Warmly.)* Many thanks, Robert. *(Artinian goes off L. Jensen is about to stay when Hockstader stops him.)*

HOCKSTADER.  Bill, I want you to myself a minute. *(Jensen exits L.)* Now what's this I hear about you not goin' on the TV?

RUSSELL.  I can't.

HOCKSTADER.  How the hell you goin to fight this thing if you don't?

RUSSELL.  Dr. Artinian ...

HOCKSTADER.  *(Disgust.)* Dr. Artinian! That's just *one* doctor. They'll say he's a friend of yours. Cantwell's going to insist they have half the medical profession look you over between now and tomorrow ... *(Pacing, happily.)* Oh, I tell you, Bill, I feel wonderful! Up all night ... on the go all morning, seein' delegates ... I tell you there is *nothin'* like a dirty lowdown political fight to put the roses in your cheeks.

RUSSELL.  *(Concerned.)* How *do* you feel?

HOCKSTADER. Immortal! Now a lot of the delegates know that somethin's up. They don't know what ...

RUSSELL. *(Abruptly.)* Art, why didn't you endorse me last night?

HOCKSTADER. *(Awkwardly.)* Look, Bill, this isn't easy to say, but you might as well know: I came to Philadelphia to nominate Cantwell.

RUSSELL. *(Nods.)* I knew that.

HOCKSTADER. *(Taken aback.)* You did! How?

RUSSELL. *(Wryly.)* Prince Hamlet has second sight. He sees motives as well as ghosts upon the battlement.

HOCKSTADER. Guess I ain't as sly as I figured I was.

RUSSELL. Did you decide to help me now because of what Joe's doing? Bringing up that breakdown business?

HOCKSTADER. No. No. Matter of fact ... speaking as a professional politician ... I kind of admire what he's doing. It's clever as all hell. No, Joe Cantwell lost me because he wasn't smart. He made a mistake. He figured I was goin' to back you when I wasn't. You got my message. Joe didn't. Now that's a serious error. Shows he don't understand character and a president if he don't understand anything else has got to understand people. Then he got flustered when I needled him. A president don't get flustered when a man gives him the needle. He keeps a straight face, like poker. *(Smiles.)* Like you're doin' right now. But what does Joe do? He don't run scared; he runs terrified. He fires off a cannon to kill a bug. And that is just plain dumb and I mean to knock him off ... which means that you, I guess, are goin to be our next President.

RUSSELL. President ... but by default. Because you still have your doubts about me, don't you?

HOCKSTADER. Yes, I still have my doubts. Bill, I want a strong president ...

RUSSELL. An immoral president? *(Hockstader turns away disgustedly.)*

HOCKSTADER. They hardly come in any other size.

RUSSELL. You don't believe that ... *(Jensen enters with a plump, bald, nervous man of forty-odd who resembles an unmade studio couch.)*

JENSEN. This is Sheldon Marcus.

HOCKSTADER. *(Irritably.)* Who the hell is Sheldon Marcus?

*(Hockstader turns, sees that the man is already in the room; he flashes a presidential smile and, hand outstretched, crosses to Marcus.)* If you'll excuse me, sir?

MARCUS. That's all right. I ... I never thought I'd meet a president. *(Marcus rubs his shaken hand against his trouser leg.)* My hands sweat. I ... I'm nervous, I guess. You see, I just now came in from Wilmington, where I live, outside Wilmington's actually where I live, a suburb you never heard of called ...

RUSSELL. Dick, what's this all about? I'm Bill Russell.

JENSEN. Mr. Marcus served in the army with Joe Cantwell ...

HOCKSTADER. In the army? *(Starts to beam with anticipation.)* Ah ... ah ... *Now* we're gettin' somewhere. Well, what was it? Was he a member of the Ku Klux Klan? The Communist Party? Or did he run away when the guns went off?

MARCUS. Well, sir, Mr. President, sir, uh, we weren't anywheres around where there were guns ...

JENSEN. They were both in the Aleutians. On the island of Adak. The Quartermaster Corps.

MARCUS. *(Nods.)* We were there for a year, well, maybe more like eighteen months for me and, oh, maybe sixteen, seventeen months for Joe, he came there February '43 and I got there ...

RUSSELL. *(To Jensen.)* Dick, what are you trying to prove?

HOCKSTADER. Now shush, Bill. And let's hear the dirt, whatever it is.

MARCUS. Well ... Joe ... *(Pauses in an agony of embarrassment.)* Oh, I sure hate talking about him, telling something so awful ...

JENSEN. I had a lead on this months ago. I finally tracked it down ... Tell them, Mr. Marcus.

MARCUS. Well, Joe Cantwell was a captain and I was a captain and Joe Cantwell was ... was ... well, he was ... you know how it is sometimes when there's all those men together and ... and ...

JENSEN. And no female companionship ...

MARCUS. That's right, though we had some nurses later on, but not enough to make much difference. I mean there were all those men ...

JENSEN. *(Helpfully.)* And no women.

RUSSELL. *(Irritated.)* Oh, for Christ's sake, Dick, stop it, will you?

HOCKSTADER. *(Soothingly.)* Now ... now, let's not get ahead of ourselves.

RUSSELL. You know Joe isn't that, and if he was, so what?

HOCKSTADER. I find this very interesting. Mr. Marcus ... Captain Marcus, I should say ...

MARCUS. *(Gabbling.)* I was a major, actually, promoted just before my discharge in '46. I'm in the reserve ... the *in*active reserve ... but if there was another war I would be ...

HOCKSTADER. *(Through him.)* Major Marcus, am I to understand by the way you are beating slowly around the bush that Joe Cantwell is what ... when I was a boy ... we called a degenerate?

MARCUS. *(Relieved to have the word said.)* Yes, sir, Mr. President, sir, that's just what I mean ...

RUSSELL. *(Amused in spite of himself.)* I don't believe it! Nobody with that awful wife and those ugly children could be anything but normal!

HOCKSTADER. Bill! Patience. Whether *you* believe it or not is beside the point.

RUSSELL. And even if it were true I'm damned if I'd smear him with something like that.

HOCKSTADER. *(Patiently and slowly.)* Bill, I, like you, am a tolerant man. I *personally* do not care if Joe Cantwell enjoys deflowering sheep by the light of a full moon. But I am interested in finding a way to stop him cold.

RUSSELL. Damn it, Art, this is exactly the kind of thing I went into politics to stop! The business of gossip instead of issues, personalities instead of policies ... We've got enough on Cantwell's *public* life to defeat him without going into his private life, which is nobody's business!

HOCKSTADER. *(Sharply.)* Any more than yours is?

RUSSELL. Any more than mine is.

HOCKSTADER. But Cantwell *is* using your private life ...

RUSSELL. All the more reason for my *not* using his. I'm not Cantwell.

HOCKSTADER. *(Reasonably.)* But nobody's used anything *yet.*

RUSSELL. Look here, Art, you are *not* my campaign manager. I am the one running for president, not you. *(To Jensen, grimly.)* And as for you, Dick ...

JENSEN. *(Growing desperate.)* Bill, at least *listen* to the man.

RUSSELL. No!

HOCKSTADER. I'm beginning to wonder if maybe I'm tryin' to help the wrong team.

RUSSELL. *(Losing control.)* Perhaps you are. Perhaps you'd be happier with Cantwell, helping him throw his mud! *(A tense silence. Hockstader remains impassive. Russell recovers himself quickly. He is contrite.)* Art, I'm sorry. I didn't mean that.

HOCKSTADER. *(Amused.)* Observe how I kept a straight face while being insulted?

RUSSELL. You know that I only meant ...

HOCKSTADER. *(Through him.)* Yes, I know. *(Wheedling.)* Now, Bill, as a favor to an old man in his ... sunset years, will you just listen to Major Marcus? That's all. Just listen.

RUSSELL. All right, Art. I'll listen. But only as a favor to ... to a friend.

HOCKSTADER. That's fine, Bill. You just relax now and let events take their course. *(Hockstader crosses to the dazed Marcus.)* After all, how often does a million dollars drop in your lap? Not to mention the presidency. *(Propels Marcus to the sofa.)* Sit down, Major Marcus, sit down. Please. Make yourself comfortable. Fact, I will mix you a drink myself with these old skilled fingers, and while I do you will tell us your story. *(Crosses to bar.)* Omitting no details, no matter how sordid.

MARCUS. Well, Mr. President, there was this guy up on Adak, and his name was Fenn, Bob Fenn. That is, *Robert* Fenn. *(Lights start to fade.)* I don't know his middle initial but I guess it's all there in the record, how this Lieutenant Fenn ...

## Curtain

48

# ACT TWO

## Scene 1

*The Cantwell suite. A few minutes later. Mabel, Alice and Mrs. Gamadge sit in a row on the sofa in the living room. Mrs. Gamadge is in a long evening dress with a vast corsage. Reporters and cameramen are winding up a press conference. Blades hovers, directs.*

BLADES. All right, boys ... come on ... that's enough ... our girls have got a lot to do ...

REPORTER 1. Mrs. Russell, where are your sons now?

ALICE. They ... well, one's in Watch Hill and the other's traveling ... he's in Europe. I wish now we had them here, for the experience. *(A flashbulb goes off.)*

MABEL. Oh, I blinked my eyes! *(To Reporter 1 gaily.)* Joe and I were going to bring our girls to Philadelphia but then we decided, no, this sort of thing is just too hectic for children ...

REPORTER 2. Mrs. Russell ... how's *Mr.* Russell today?

ALICE. He's just fine ...

REPORTER 3. There has been a rumor that he is not in the very best of health.

ALICE. *(Growing steely.)* I have never seen him in better health.

MABEL. My Joe just blossoms during a campaign! On the go all the time! I don't know *where* he gets the energy.

ALICE. In fact, my husband ...

MRS. GAMADGE. *(Through her.)* Joe Cantwell is a real dynamo!

ALICE. *(A second try.)* In fact, my husband ...

MABEL. I sometimes think Joe has got nerves of iron. Nothing ever seems to upset him.

MRS. GAMADGE. *(Nods.)* He has a great inner calm, which is almost spiritual.

49

ALICE. *(Gamely.)* My husband …

BLADES. OK. That's it, fellows … *(The reporters start to go.)*

REPORTER 3. *(To Alice.)* What do you think's going to happen tomorrow? Do you think Mr. Russell's got it on the first ballot?

ALICE. I certainly hope so!

MABEL. *(Butter would not melt, etc.)* Well, as for me, I just hope the best man wins! I mean for the country and everything.

MRS. GAMADGE. Amen to that! *(Blades follows the reporters out right through the office.)*

BLADES. Good day, ladies! *(The three women are alone. Mabel and Mrs. Gamadge immediately light up cigarettes.)*

MABEL. Well, *that* was an ordeal, wasn't it, Mrs. Russell?

ALICE. I'm sure it wasn't for you. *(Afraid this sounded too sharp, amends.)* I mean you've done so much of this … kind of thing. *(Rises.)* I have to go. *(Mabel gets to her feet quickly.)*

MABEL. Oh, stay and have a drink … just for a minute. I don't have anything to do till *(Looks at schedule.)* … till four-fifteen. So let's play hooky!

ALICE. I'm afraid I have an appointment in fifteen minutes.

MRS. GAMADGE. They have us girls on timetables just like trains. Will you look at me? *(She rises.)* All ready to moderate the fashion show at five o'clock.

MABEL. *(Cozily.)* It's a shame we couldn't do everything together, instead of first you meetin' one group and then me meetin' the same group … What can I fix you? *(Mabel makes herself a martini.)*

ALICE. Nothing, thanks. It's too early for me.

MRS. GAMADGE. Well, didn't Art Hockstader surprise everybody last night?

MABEL. Personally, I think he's an old meanie the way he's holding out. And you know why? Publicity! He absolutely revels in the limelight … Oh, Mrs. Russell, I don't believe you've seen my children.

ALICE. I've seen pictures of them. They're very … pretty. *(Mabel holds up a photograph. Mrs. Gamadge crosses to the desk for a newspaper, then joins the women looking at the photograph.)*

MABEL. That's Gladys there, the oldest … with the braces on her teeth. I'm afraid they're all going to have to have braces and Lord knows *where* they got those teeth from. Both Joe and I have perfect teeth, and oh! what a fortune it is having children's teeth straightened! Do you have a picture of your boys?

ALICE. No. Not with me ...

MRS. GAMADGE. So good-looking ...

MABEL. Yes! That was a nice spread on them in *Life*. Such *warm* pictures! You and Mr. Russell certainly get a lot of coverage from *Life*, much more than we do.

ALICE. Oh? I thought we were neck and neck.

MABEL. No. I'm afraid Joe and I must simply forget Mr. Luce. You're *his* candidate. For the time being. Oh, come on, sit down. *(Alice and Mabel sit on the sofa, Mrs. Gamadge sits in the chair.)* I do like the way you do your hair.

ALICE. Oh? Well ...

MABEL. You look so like this English teacher I had at State College. A wonderful woman in every way ...

ALICE. Thank you. But I'm afraid I'm not wonderful ...

MABEL. Now ... no false modesty! You are wonderful *and* courageous. I always say Alice Russell is the most courageous woman in public life, don't I, Sue-Ellen? *(Mrs. Gamadge, immersed in her paper, nods.)*

ALICE. *(Curiously.)* In what way, courageous?

MABEL. Why, that committee you were on!

MRS. GAMADGE. *(Suddenly alert.)* Committee? *What* committee?

MABEL. *(Ready for the kill.)* You know — in New York City, the one where you did all that work for *birth control*.

MRS. GAMADGE. *(Horror.)* Birth control! I didn't know that.

ALICE. Well, it *was* twenty years ago. And of course I'm not supposed to mention it now ... *(To Mabel.)* as *you* know.

MRS. GAMADGE. I should hope not! You'll have the Catholics down on us like a ton of bricks. The rhythm cycle, yes *(Makes a vague circular motion with her hand.)* but anything else ... is out.

MABEL. Of course I'm against any kind of artificial means of birth control except where it's a matter of health maybe, but believe me I think it took the courage of a lion to be in favor of people using these contraceptive things when you're in public life. Of course I guess you didn't know then your husband would be running for president one day and when you do that you just can't afford to offend a lot of nice people who vote.

ALICE. I realize that. We must offend no one. Of course, if you offend no one, you don't please anyone very much either, do you? But I suppose that is an occupational hazard in politics. We are all interchangeably inoffensive. *(There is a pause.)*

MRS. GAMADGE. Well, now!

MABEL. *(Overlapping.)* Well, hooray for Mrs. Russell! Do you know, you sounded just like your husband then? Didn't she, Sue-Ellen? Didn't she sound Just like Bill Russell when he's being witty and profound and way over our poor heads!

ALICE. I'd like to think intelligence was contagious. But I'm afraid it isn't, at least in my case. Bill has the brains. I'm not awfully quick.

MABEL. Oh, yes, you are, honey!

ALICE. I've really got to go. *(Alice rises, starts to the corridor door. Mabel follows her.)*

MRS. GAMADGE. You girls are an absolute inspiration to the American woman, *and I mean it* ... each in your different way.

ALICE. Thank you very much ... for that.

MABEL. *(One last shot.)* Oh, by the way, how *is* Mr. Russell's health? I mean *really?* I thought he looked so peaked last night at the dinner and someone did say ...

ALICE. *(Grimly.)* The reporters are gone, Mrs. Cantwell. You know as well as I do he's perfectly all right. Goodbye.

MRS. GAMADGE. Bye. *(Alice goes.)*

MABEL. Well ... listen to her! "The reporters are gone, Mrs. Cantwell!" If she wasn't so high and mighty she'd take the hint and start saying right now he isn't feeling good so that when he has to pull out there'd be some preparation ... *(Mabel goes into the bedroom and flops onto the rumpled bed.)*

MRS. GAMADGE. *(Following her.)* Mabel, I don't like anything about what Joe's doing. It's plain dirty and I should warn you: I'm a loyal party worker and I'll see that the women are all behind Bill Russell.

MABEL. *Under* him is more their usual position. It's just sex, sex, sex, morning, noon and night with that Bill Russell.

MRS. GAMADGE. Now, Mabel, unless you were in the room, how would you know?

MABEL. I read that report. Bill Russell is a neurotic who has had a breakdown and his sex life is certainly not normal. Sleeping around with all those women is just plain immature. And we don't want an immature president, do we?

MRS. GAMADGE. We've had some very good presidents who have slept around a lot more than Bill Russell ever did. And in the White House, too. *(Blades, Cantwell and Carlin enter the living room from the corridor.)*

MABEL. *(Hears them.)* Here come the men!

MRS. GAMADGE. And I must get back to the women. *(She is about to leave through the corridor door when she is surprised to see Carlin. She comes into the living room.)* Hello, Senator Carlin. Didn't expect to see you *here.*

CARLIN. Just happened to be in the neighborhood. *(Cantwell comes up behind Mrs. Gamadge and kisses the back of her neck. She squeals.)*

CANTWELL. Hi, Sue-Ellen!

MRS. GAMADGE. *(Quickly recovered.)* Joe, I hope you don't mind if I take the bull by the horns and tell you right now that anything to do with *private* lives is out in politics.

CANTWELL. I couldn't agree more.

MRS. GAMADGE. That's an unwritten law and it's a good one. Once you throw at a man that he has a mistress or an illegitimate child or something like that you get sympathy for him. *(Sadly.)* I don't know why but you do. You also make yourself vulnerable because nobody's a saint. Not even you, Joe. So keep what you men do *in* bed *out* of politics. *(She goes, waving gaily.)* Bye, Joe. Bye, Clyde. Bye, Mabel.

CANTWELL. *(To Blades.)* Photostats ready?

BLADES. All neatly bound. Six hundred copies to be released to the delegates at three-thirty P.M. Russell's doctor is in town. That means there's going to be some kind of a statement.

CANTWELL. *(Nods.)* He's going to fight.

CARLIN. Aren't you fellows afraid of getting into trouble? Stealing medical records?

BLADES. *(Quickly.)* We didn't steal them.

CANTWELL. They were given to us. *Pro bono publico.* Now just look at this ... *(Cantwell shows Carlin the file. The phone rings in the living room. Mabel answers it.)*

MABEL. Yes? Who? Oh, Dick Jensen! Yes, Joe's here. Just a sec. You hold on now. *(To Cantwell, excited.)* This is it, honey! They're giving up!

CANTWELL. *(Takes phone.)* Hi, Dick. How's a boy? Fine ... Well, gosh, I don't see how I can delay much longer. I've told everybody three-thirty. Of course I'd sort of hoped Bill would be helpful. You know, for the Party's sake. He could back out so easily now, on this health issue ... Yeah? Well, frankly, I don't see any point to postponing ... Do I know who? Shel-don Mar-cus? No, I don't think so ... *Where? (Harshly.)* I want to see Russell. Right now ... Well, try and fix it; I'll be right here. *(He hangs up, frowning.)*

MABEL. Well, honey, what did he say? Come on now ... give with the T.L.!

BLADES. *(Concerned.)* You aren't going to meet with Russell, are you? I thought we'd decided.

CANTWELL. Hold that stuff on Russell.

BLADES. Hold it? But we can't. We promised the delegates, three-thirty, we said ...

CANTWELL. I said hold it.

MABEL. *(Alarm.)* Joe, what's happening? *(Cantwell takes the file from Carlin.)*

CANTWELL. Senator, if you'll excuse me ...

CARLIN. Oh, sure ... sure ... Well, goodbye, Mrs. Cantwell. *(At the door, he turns to Cantwell.)* You know where to find me ... *after* three-thirty. *(Carlin goes.)*

CANTWELL. *(To Blades.)* Go on, stop that release.

BLADES. *(Bewildered.)* OK ... you're the boss. *(Blades goes off R. Cantwell goes into bedroom. He sits down on the bed, thinking hard. Mabel follows, panic beginning.)*

MABEL. Joe, what did Russell say to you? What's he doing to you? *(Cantwell looks at her blankly. Mabel begins to understand.)* It's not ... it's not ... *(Mabel stops. Slowly, Cantwell nods. Mabel, horrified, sits beside him on the bed, her arm around him. Softly:)* Oh, my God!

# Scene 2

*The Russell suite. A few minutes later. Marcus has just fin-*
*ished his story. Russell stands downstage right, Hockstader*
*starts to rise from the chair to give Marcus the Cantwell file*
*he has been studying but drops it on the floor. He sits back*
*suddenly. Marcus picks up the file. Jensen is hanging up the*
*phone as the lights come up.*

JENSEN. *(Excitedly.)* You should've heard Cantwell's voice! First
time I've ever heard him stuck! *(To Russell.)* He wants to see you.
So I said three-thirty and he agreed without a peep. That means *no*
announcement to the delegates. *(Russell turns and crosses to Marcus,*
*who rises.)*
RUSSELL. Mr. Marcus, I want to thank you. I know that all this
must be as ... distasteful to you as it is to us. *(Russell shakes Marcus'*
*hand.)*
MARCUS. Well, yes, it is ... Peggy, my wife, oh, she was fit to be
tied when I said I'd talked to Mr. Jensen and was going to come
here and see you. She knew the whole story of course. I tell her
everything, we have no secrets, Mrs. Marcus and me ... *(Russell*
*talks through him as he tries to get him off L.)*
RUSSELL. Yes ... yes ... well, many thanks.
JENSEN. *(To Marcus.)* Would you wait ... please? In my office?
That's the second room, across the hall.
MARCUS. Yes, sir, Mr. Jensen. *(To Hockstader.)* I guess this is the
biggest moment of my life, meeting you, Mr. President, sir.
*(Hockstader, seated, shakes his hand.)*
HOCKSTADER. I expect this *is* the biggest moment of your life,
Major. You may have changed history. Excuse me for not getting
up. *(Marcus is now beginning to enjoy the situation.)*
MARCUS. I'll say one thing, I certainly never thought back in '44
when Joe Cantwell and I were on Adak that sixteen years later we'd
be here in this hotel with him running for president and me talking

to you, sir, who I always admired, *(Confidentially.)* though I didn't vote for you the second time. You see, Mrs. Marcus felt that ...

HOCKSTADER. *(Dulcet tones.)* Let your vote, Major Marcus, remain between you and your god.

MARCUS. *(Overcome by this wisdom.)* I guess that's right. Yes. Yes! I'll remember that, sir, I really will ... *(To Jensen, at door.)* I won't have to see Joe, will I?

JENSEN. We hope not.

MARCUS. He's just awful when he's mad ... he's got this temper. It's like stepping on a snake, stepping on Joe. He can be real scary. *(Jensen gets him through the door at last.)*

JENSEN. We'll remember that. Thanks a lot. See you in a few minutes ... *(To Russell.)* Bill, we've done it! We've stopped Joe Cantwell!

RUSSELL. *(Indicates a folder on the coffee table in front of Hockstader.)* I'm not going to use this.

JENSEN. *(Quickly.)* Of course you're not. Except privately. We just take this to Joe and say: "If you make an issue out of this breakdown, *we* make an issue out of a certain bit of court-martial testimony ... " *(Alice enters from corridor.)*

RUSSELL. Alice, how did it go?

ALICE. My cheeks are tired from smiling for the camera. *(To Hockstader.)* But I must say. I'm beginning to like politics, Mr. President, especially when Mrs. Gamadge tells me that I'm an inspiration to American women ... in my way.

HOCKSTADER. You're an inspiration to me, Miss Alice. Excuse me for not getting up, but would you fetch me some branch water, some just *plain* branch water?

ALICE. Of course. *(Alice goes to the bar.)* Well, first we talked about Mabel's children. Then we talked about *my* children. Then we discussed the role of women in politics. We both agreed that woman's true place was in the home.

RUSSELL. I'm sure Mrs. Gamadge was eloquent on that subject.

ALICE. Eloquent to the point of obsession. We also agreed that women should be informed about issues.

HOCKSTADER. Worst damn thing ever happened to this country, giving the women the vote. Trouble, trouble, trouble. They got no more sense than a bunch of geese. Give 'em a big smile and a pinch on the ... anatomy and you got ten votes.

ALICE. *(Smiles.)* May I quote you, Mr. President?

HOCKSTADER. I will deny ever having made such a vile and un-American statement. *(Takes glass.)* Thank you, ma'am.

ALICE. *(To Russell.)* And, finally, there were some pointed references to your health ...

RUSSELL. Which means they've started. Mentally unstable. Apt to crack up ... already showing signs of the strain. *(Sighs.)* As a matter of fact, I *am* showing signs of strain. *(Jensen holds up the folder.)*

JENSEN. Bill, you can stop them. Right now. We've got the ultimate weapon, massive retaliation as Foster Dulles used to say. *(Woman aide opens door at L.; she whispers something to Jensen, who nods. She goes. Jensen beams.)* We have a visitor. *(Blades enters, simulating jauntiness.)*

BLADES. Gentlemen ... Mr. President! *(Hockstader ignores him.)*

RUSSELL. Mr. Blades, contrary to what you may have been told, I'm *not* seeing Joe Cantwell.

BLADES. Oh? But I thought you were. I thought Joe said you'd meet in his room because there aren't so many reporters down there ...

JENSEN. *(To Russell.)* That's right, Bill. I said we'd be right down ...

RUSSELL. You did! *(Blades studies every nuance, trying to get a sense of what is happening.)*

BLADES. So I came up to work out some way of getting the Secretary downstairs without anybody seeing him. I checked the service elevator and ...

HOCKSTADER. Dick, you and that hatchet man there go try out the bathroom route. Through the bedroom. Into the next suite and on down.

BLADES. *(Probing.)* OK, Mr. President, but if the Secretary *isn't* going downstairs ...

HOCKSTADER. *(Cold command.)* Get moving, boys. *(Jensen indicates for Blades to go with him.)*

JENSEN. Come on, Don. This is the dry run. *(Reluctantly, Blades follows Jensen into the bathroom by way of the bedroom.)*

RUSSELL. *(To Hockstader.)* I'm not going to do this.

HOCKSTADER. You have to.

ALICE. Do what?

HOCKSTADER. He's got the stuff to knock off Cantwell. Only your lily-livered husband won't go through with it.

ALICE. *(To Russell.)* You can keep them from bringing up all that ... mental business?

RUSSELL. Maybe ...

HOCKSTADER. Definitely.

ALICE. Then do it!

RUSSELL. But you don't know what it is I have to do.

ALICE. *(Fiercely.)* I don't care! If you took a gun and shot him I'd help you if I thought that was the only way of keeping our lives ... private.

HOCKSTADER. Atta girl! Listen to her, Bill. *She* don't run from a fight.

RUSSELL. You know I'm not afraid.

HOCKSTADER. *(Exasperation.)* Then what is wrong with you? Why are you hesitatin' *this* time?

RUSSELL. Look, I'm not being righteous and I'm not being fastidious and I do want to win. But how can I, in all conscience, use ... *this,* even against Cantwell!

HOCKSTADER. *(Furiously.)* I should've stuck with Cantwell! Because listenin' to you hem and haw and talk about your conscience is turnin' me against you fast. My God, what would happen if you had to make a quick decision in the White House when maybe all our lives depended on whether you could act fast ... and you just sat there, the way you're doin' now, having a high old time with your divided conscience.

RUSSELL. *(Hotly.)* I am *not* divided! I know what I should do and this is *not* it.

HOCKSTADER. Then you don't want to be king of the castle. So stay away from us. Be a saint on your own time. Because you aren't fit to lead anybody.

RUSSELL. *(Stung.)* Why? Because I don't "fire off a cannon to kill a bug"? Because I don't have that quick mindless reaction you seem to confuse with strength? Well, I promise you, there is more danger in a president who acts on animal reflex than in one who is willing to reflect before he acts, who has some vestigial moral sense that goes beyond himself. Don't you see? If I start to fight like Cantwell I lose all meaning ...

HOCKSTADER. *(Evenly.)* If you don't start to fight, you are finished. Now I am here to tell you this: Power is not a toy we give to good children; it is a weapon and the strong man takes it and he uses it and I can assure you he don't turn it on himself nor let another man come at him with a knife that he don't fight back. Well, that knife is at your throat and if you don't go down there and beat Cantwell to the floor with this very dirty stick, then you got no business in this big league, and bastard or not I'll help Joe Cantwell take the whole damned world if he wants it, because it's not for you and never will be! *(A long moment, broken by the return of Jensen and Blades from the bathroom R.)*

JENSEN. Well, the coast is clear. We're all set.

BLADES. First, we pass through a suite containing a hosiery salesman and a woman ... perhaps not his wife.

JENSEN. Definitely not his wife. *(To Russell.)* He looks forward to meeting you even though he hopes Cantwell gets the nomination. His companion betrayed no intimacy with the names of either candidate.

BLADES. Then we go down the back stairs and through a room occupied by a widow from Bangor, Maine, who is for Russell ...

JENSEN. And from there we go to the Cantwell bathroom and then ... they meet and make history!

BLADES. That's right! Though what's going on beats me. *(Hockstader has been eyeing Russell coldly during this.)*

HOCKSTADER. *(To Russell, softly.)* Here's your chance. Your *last* chance. Take it. Go down there. I want a strong president to keep us alive a while longer. *(Russell makes his decision. He turns to Blades and Jensen. He motions toward the bedroom.)*

RUSSELL. Wait for me in there.

BLADES. *(As he goes.)* How are you feeling, Mr. President?

HOCKSTADER. *(Grimly.)* Just fine, considering the alternative. *(Chuckling, Blades joins Jensen at the bathroom door. Russell picks up the documents.)*

RUSSELL. *(Half to himself.)* And so, one by one, these compromises, these small corruptions destroy character.

HOCKSTADER. To want power is corruption already. Dear God, you hate yourself for being human.

RUSSELL. No. I only want to *be* human ... and it is not easy.

Once this sort of thing starts, there is no end to it which is why it should never begin. And if *I* start, well, Art, how does it end, this sort of thing? *Where* does it end?

HOCKSTADER.   In the grave, son, where the dust is neither good nor bad, but just nothing. *(Russell looks first at Hockstader, then at Alice. He goes into the bedroom. Alice follows him; she pauses at the door and watches as Russell. exits to the bathroom, where Jensen and Blades are waiting.)*

ALICE.   *(Slowly.)* You are a good man, Mr. President.

HOCKSTADER.   I reckon I am, when all's said and done. *(Hockstader, in pain, tries to take one of his pills; he cannot get his hand to his mouth.)*

ALICE.   But I don't know if this is the right thing for Bill to do. *(Alice continues to look after Russell, unaware of Hockstader's pain.)*

HOCKSTADER.   At least I put a fire under the candidate. I just hope it don't go out ... Now don't you get alarmed *(Alice turns on this, startled.)* but I want you to go over and pick up that phone and ask for Dr. Latham, he's in the hotel. Tell him I'm in here ... tell him to come quick, through the back way. Tell him to bring a stretcher because I can't move. *(Alice, horrified, goes quickly to the telephone.)* I'm afraid the old man is just about dead.

## Scene 3

*The Cantwell suite. A moment later. Cantwell is on the telephone in the living room. Mabel is beside him. Both wait, nervously.*

CANTWELL.   *(At last.)* Yes, that's right. The name is Conyers, General Conyers ... C-o-n-y-e-r-s ... Yes, this is Senator Cantwell. Yes, it's an emergency. You ... What? Oh, no! *(To Mabel.)* They can't find him!

MABEL.   But he *has* to be there!

CANTWELL.   *(Into telephone.)* Try his quarters, then. *(Softly, to himself.)* Damnit, damnit, damnit.

MABEL. Are you sure General Conyers will back you up?

CANTWELL. He better. *(Into telephone.)* Well, isn't there a phone anywhere near there? *(To Mabel.)* He's playing golf! *(Into telephone.)* OK. Tell him as soon as you find him to call Senator Cantwell, in Philadelphia. The number is Walnut 8-7593 ... Got it? Thank you. *(Cantwell puts the receiver down; he rises, starts to pace, thinking hard.)*

MABEL. But you've *got* to talk to him before they come down here.

CANTWELL. It's too late now. *(Thoughtfully.)* Maybe it's just as well ... *(Starts to plan.)* Now, let's see: Conyers ... the delegates ... Sheldon Marcus. *(Slowly.)* Yes, Sheldon Marcus ...

MABEL. Joe, I am scared to death ...

CANTWELL. Well, don't be. *(Soothingly.)* Come here, poor Mama Bear. *(He embraces her.)* And don't worry. Poppa Bear isn't going to get shot down this close to the honey-tree.

MABEL. I just don't know how they can use something like that which is so untrue, which is a dirty lie and everybody knew it was a lie even at the time ... Oh, how I hate politics! *(The telephone rings. Cantwell breaks away to answer it.)*

CANTWELL. Conyers! *(Into telephone.)* Yes? Who? *(Startled.)* Oh, Mrs. Russell ... Yes, this is Joe Cantwell ... No, Bill isn't here yet. I guess he's still on his way down ... *What?* Oh, that's awful! And you say he's ... Yes, of course. Of course I'll tell Bill. The second he gets here. Yes ... He's a great guy. Yes, thank you. Goodbye, Mrs. Russell. *(Puts down the receiver.)* Art Hockstader just collapsed. They've taken him to the hospital. He's dying.

MABEL. Dying? I thought he ...

CANTWELL. That hernia stuff was a lot of bull.

MABEL. But what's this going to do to us, his dying now?

CANTWELL. Find out what hospital he's at. *(Russell, Blades and Jensen emerge from the bathroom into the bedroom. Cantwell hears them. He gestures warningly to Mabel, who is about to exit R.)* Not a word about Hockstader. I don't want anything to upset this meeting. *(Cantwell gets himself into position as the three men enter the living room.)*

BLADES. Well, here we are!

JENSEN. Touch and go for a while there but we made it. Nobody saw us. *(Russell and Cantwell stare at one another curiously. A long silence.)*

MABEL. *(Gaily.)* Well, now, will you look at that! I tell you they look just like two wild animals in the zoo! *(Pause.)* Well, come on now ... somebody *say* something! It's just politics, that's all, isn't like the end of the world or anything ...

JENSEN. *(Flatly.)* Yet.

MABEL. I had such a nice visit with your wife, Mr. Russell ... and she is getting to be a real campaigner, isn't she? *(Starts to cross to bar.)* Could I fix you a drink or something? We have just about everything. Let me see, there's gin and there's Scotch and there's bourbon with branch water like President Hockstader always used to ... *(She stops of her own accord, remembering.)*

CANTWELL. I don't think we want a drink, Mabel.

RUSSELL. No, thank you.

MABEL. *(To Blades.)* Well, in that case I believe we must make ourselves scarce, Don.

BLADES. *(To Russell.)* Let me know when you're ready to go back upstairs. *(Blades exits R.)*

CANTWELL. *(To Russell.)* Is Sheldon Marcus in the hotel?

JENSEN. Yes.

CANTWELL. Could I see him? *(To Russell.)* I'd like to ask him some questions ... in front of you, if it's all right. *(Russell nods.)*

JENSEN. I'll bring him down.

CANTWELL. *(Indicates office to R.)* Have him wait in there. *(Jensen goes off L.)*

MABEL. Well, I guess you two boys want to be alone. *(To Russell.)* Now you go easy on my Joe ... who is the best husband that ever was, ever! Well, goodbye, now ... *(To Cantwell, nervously.)* Joe honey, if you want me I'll be over in Sue-Ellen Gamadge's room, we're having a real old-time hen fest this afternoon, with all the governors' wives ... *(Cantwell nods to her, encouragingly. Mabel exits through office.)*

CANTWELL. Well, Bill, here we are ... the main event, like they say.

RUSSELL. The main event. And here we stand, as Martin Luther said ...

CANTWELL. *(Misunderstanding.)* Oh, I'm sorry ... sit down, please ...

RUSSELL. And it is not safe to move.

CANTWELL. Who said what?

RUSSELL. Martin Luther said: It is not safe to move. *(Explaining.)* Luther was …

CANTWELL. *(Irritably.)* You don't need to tell me who Martin Luther was. I happen to be a Protestant. I'm a very religious kind of guy … Bill.

RUSSELL. *(Ironically.)* You don't need to tell *me* that … Joe. *(Russell sits on the sofa D. Cantwell remains standing.)*

CANTWELL. *(Stung.)* You really do think you're better than all of us, with your bad jokes, and the admiration of a lot of bleeding-heart fellow travelers and would-be intellectuals who don't mean a thing in this country!

RUSSELL. *(Appreciatively.)* That was very good, Joe. Pure Cantwell. Known as the multiple lie. Or in this case the multiple-lie-plus-confused-statement. For instance, you say that I think I'm better than the rest of you …

CANTWELL. *(Quickly.)* You don't deny …

RUSSELL. *(Chuckling.)* Excellent. Interrupt before the answer begins. That's vintage Cantwell …

CANTWELL. *(District-attorney voice.)* I'm not interested in your sophistry. Your contempt. Your deliberate refusal to answer …

RUSSELL. *(Bangs ashtray on coffee table.)* Mr. Chairman! Mr. Chairman! Point of order! *(Laughs.)* Oh, how're you going to keep them down in the Senate once they've been on TV?

CANTWELL. *(Smiles.)* Very funny. Very cute. I like that. You should have your own TV show.

RUSSELL. Thank you. I'm sure you meant that as a compliment … Joe, I came down here to convince you that there are some things a man cannot do even in politics … *(Cantwell sits opposite him D.)*

CANTWELL. *(Not listening.)* Now I have given you every hint, every opportunity in the past two days to pull out of the race. Considering your medical history, it could be done so easily … so logically. All you'd have to do is claim exhaustion, fatigue … like the last time … and then this ugly business would never come up and the Party could then unite behind its candidate …

RUSSELL. You?

CANTWELL. *(Nods.)* And we take the election in November.

RUSSELL. You make it sound so simple, but it isn't. For one thing, you'll be sued for the theft of my case history.

CANTWELL. *(Tries to interrupt.)* Bill …

RUSSELL. But that's not the point.

CANTWELL. *(Again.)* Bill …

RUSSELL. What I want you to realize …

CANTWELL. *(Voice of reason.)* Bill! I didn't steal it. The thing was *given* to me, unsolicited. Anyway, I'm sure your doctor won't file suit if you ask him not to.

RUSSELL. *(Taken aback.)* Why should I ask him not to?

CANTWELL. *(Promptly.)* Party unity. What's the point of smearing me when I'm the one who's got to get us into the White House?

RUSSELL. What makes you so certain *you're* going to be nominated?

CANTWELL. *(As to a child.)* Because I expect you to withdraw … because you've got no choice. Then who else is there? Except me.

RUSSELL. *(Stunned.)* You are … amazing! I came down here with enough political nitroglycerine not only to knock you out of the race but out of politics altogether, and there you sit and blandly tell me *I'm* the one to withdraw.

CANTWELL. *(Through him.)* I also promise to use you, once I'm elected. And that's a solemn promise, Bill. You can have any post in the cabinet you want, excepting Secretary of State, where I'm all hung up with somebody else. Or you can go as our first ambassador to Red China … *(Russell looks at him, amazed.)* That's right. You'll be happy to know I intend to recognize Red China, though I won't make an issue of it until public opinion is more …

RUSSELL. *(Thoughtfully.)* Never defend, always attack. You're very good at this, Joe. I mean that.

CANTWELL. Another thing you ought to know since you've made such a point about it in your attacks on me: Politically we are almost the same on every important issue. *Only* I am less reckless than you. I believe in timing. I don't see anything to be gained by launching a policy just to have it shot down maybe for good because the climate wasn't right.

RUSSELL. And you call that leadership?

CANTWELL. There are many ways of leading: The worst one is making brilliant speeches on the right side at the wrong time. I know how to wait ...

RUSSELL. You are candid. *(Cantwell, bursting with energy and self-righteousness, starts to pace.)*

CANTWELL. *(Passionately.)* And I'm right! Because I was born to this. You weren't. I know in my bones how to do this thing. I understand the people of this country. Because I'm one of them. I know how to maneuver. How to win. I knew from the time I won my first election I was going to be president and nobody was going to stop me. Not even the brilliant, witty, aristocratic, intellectual William Russell, who has no more to do with the people of this county than I have to do with the Groton Harvard Wall Street set.

RUSSELL. Well, there is no immediate need to start a class war. I am not better qualified to be president because I went to Harvard than you are because you worked your way through a state college. But as you probably know there is a certain suspicion of the self-made man these days. People aren't as naive as you think. Any man who fights his way to the top is certainly to be admired, but the people sometimes wonder: How exactly did he do it? And whom did he hurt along the way? The self-made man often makes himself out of pieces of his victims. *(Russell rises and crosses to Cantwell as his own rage begins.)* You are something of a Frankenstein monster, Joe, made out of the bits and pieces of Sicilian bandits ... and your political opponents ... all assembled before our eyes on television.

CANTWELL. *(Coldly.)* How I was made is not the question. What matters is, I am here.

RUSSELL. And you think that your basic public *image* has changed?

CANTWELL. It has. According to the Gallup poll only twelve percent of the people even remember that there was a Mafia hearing.

RUSSELL. I remember.

CANTWELL. The image that they have of Cantwell is the way I am now ...

RUSSELL. Smooth, cautious, beyond reproach ...

CANTWELL. That is right. People forget. Nobody's going to get any mileage out of my past so let's get this Aleutian business over with. I'm going to question Sheldon Marcus now and you're going to get the surprise of your life. *(Russell turns away from him as he sits again on the sofa.)*

RUSSELL. Nothing *you* do ever surprises me, Joe. What I do, however, is beginning to surprise me. I never thought I could bring up something like this against any man. It revolts me …

CANTWELL. *(Generously.)* Oh, come on! Don't give it a second thought. Look, I don't blame you. I'd certainly use it against you if it was there …

RUSSELL. That's the point; *you* would. I wouldn't. Or never thought I would. *(Cantwell sees a possible break in the enemy line.)*

CANTWELL. Then what are you doing down here? What have you got this joker Marcus standing by for except to smear me as a homosexual which I'm not.

RUSSELL. *I* never said you were …

CANTWELL. *(Relentlessly.)* Then what are you doing here if you don't think I am?

RUSSELL. Had you paused at any point in your offensive, I would have told you *why* I came here and *what* I mean to do.

CANTWELL. *(Triumphantly.)* I hope you realize you have just admitted that you don't believe this accusation against me. That you are openly confessing collusion …

RUSSELL. *(Abruptly.)* Joe, shut up! *(Rises.)* Art Hockstader was right when he said you're not very sensitive to people. You're so busy trying to win you never stop to figure out *what* it is you're winning.

CANTWELL. *(Simulated weariness.)* I am only trying to stick to the issue at hand. I don't believe in indulging in personalities.

RUSSELL. Come off it, Joe! I came here to try and convince you to drop that nonsense against me just as I mean to drop this nonsense against you. These things are irrelevant and dishonest, not to mention untrue. They cancel each other out. So I wish you would please join me by *not* indulging in personalities. *(Holds up folder.)* I'll tear this up and send Sheldon Marcus back where he came from, if you drop that business against me.

CANTWELL. *(Nods.)* I see. You came here to make a deal with me.

RUSSELL. *(A sigh of exasperation.)* No! I came here to … *(Cantwell is growing confident.)*

CANTWELL. *(Warmly.)* Look, Bill, it makes perfect sense, what you're doing. And I have no hard feelings. Really, I mean it. So don't be apologetic.

RUSSELL. You have *no* feelings, I would say.

CANTWELL. And perhaps you have too many. Perhaps you *are* too emotional. The report on your breakdown said you might have thought of committing suicide …

RUSSELL. Who hasn't thought of it?

CANTWELL. I never have. And I don't think a president should. No matter how tough the going is.

RUSSELL. *(Amused.)* Am I to understand you want to save the country from me? That you are genuinely afraid I'm unstable?

CANTWELL. Yes, I am. You just admitted you thought of suicide …

RUSSELL. Then, Joe, if I'm so unstable, why did you offer me the ambassadorship to Red China?

CANTWELL. *(Promptly.)* The president can keep tabs on an ambassador. Nobody can keep tabs on a president.

RUSSELL. *(Nods.)* Never pause for an answer, in the best tradition of a television performer … Well, let's get this dirty business over with. I won't throw my mud if you won't throw your mud.

CANTWELL. And we go into the convention tomorrow and you get nominated on the first ballot? No.

RUSSELL. Well, then … good luck. And may "the best man" win, assuming we don't knock each other off *and* the Party. *(Russell turns to go. Cantwell signals frantically.)*

CANTWELL. Now wait a minute … Wait a minute! Bill! I realize we've got to work something out. And I'm willing to be reasonable, only you have *got* to …

RUSSELL. *(Exploding.)* Stop it! Either we declare a moratorium on mud or we both let fly. *(Swiftly Cantwell shifts his tack. He goes to door at R.)*

CANTWELL. OK. *(Opens the door, looks through into office.)* Don, send Mr. Marcus in. *(To Russell.)* Can I see that court-martial testimony? *(Russell gives him the testimony. He studies it as Marcus enters, nervously. A long moment. Then Cantwell speaks, still studying documents.)* Hi, Shelly, how's the boy? Long time no see.

MARCUS. Yeah … Joe … long time … Hello again, Mr. Russell.

RUSSELL. Joe wants to ask you some questions …

MARCUS. Well, I really ought to be getting back to Wilmington, you see, my wife …

CANTWELL. You live in Wilmington, eh? Great town … used to have some cousins there named Everly, Jack and Helen Everly, maybe you know them, in real estate …

MARCUS. Well, it's not Wilmington proper, actually, where I live, it's a suburb where Peggy and I live. I don't think I know anybody named *(For the first time Cantwell looks at Marcus, who steps back in alarm.)* Everly …

CANTWELL. *(Smiles.)* Shelly, you put on a lot of weight.

MARCUS. Well, it's Peggy … it's my wife Peggy's cooking, she's a wonderful cook … I thought, Mr. Russell, I wouldn't have to … to …

CANTWELL. To see your old buddy? Now you know I would've been fit to be tied if I had known Shelly Marcus from Adak was in town and hadn't come to see me.

MARCUS. Well, I … I know how busy you are … *both* you men are … running for this president thing, and I was just … well passing by.

CANTWELL. *(Pleasantly.)* And you thought you would pause just long enough to smear your old buddy?

MARCUS. Now, Joe, don't get mad at me … it was … it was my duty!

CANTWELL. To get even with me for seeing you were passed over for promotion because of incompetence. *(To Russell.)* Always a good idea to start with the motive.

RUSSELL. *(To Marcus.)* Is this true?

MARCUS. *(Taken aback.)* Well, no, not really … I mean my efficiency report was …

CANTWELL. *(In for the death.)* Can be found in army records! Unsatisfactory! I was adjutant and I personally stopped his promotion *and* his transfer *and* he knew it. *(Picks up documents.)* Now, on 6 April 1944, into my quonset hut at the army base on Adak there moved a Lieutenant Fenn …

MARCUS. That was the one, like I told you … that was the one … we all knew …

CANTWELL. We shared the same hut for three months.

MARCUS. Just the two of them. Like I told you. It's all in the record there ... they were, you know ... they were ...

CANTWELL. *(Inexorably.)* Fenn was caught with an enlisted man *inflagrante delicto* on the afternoon of 14 June 1944 in the back of the post church. The M.P.s caught him ...

MARCUS. *(Rapidly.)* That's right. And that's when he broke down and told about everything and everybody ... the M.P.s laid this trap for him ... they'd been tipped off ...

CANTWELL. By the Advocate General ...

MARCUS. That's night. By Colonel Conyers, he was the one finally broke up this whole ring of degenerates ... And Fenn when he was caught gave, oh, maybe twenty, thirty names and one of those names was Joe Cantwell, his roommate ...

CANTWELL. Correct. Now: What happened to those twenty-eight officers and men who were named at the court-martial?

MARCUS. They were all separated from the service ... Section Eight we called it ... for the good of the service, they were all kicked out ...

CANTWELL. All except one.

MARCUS. That's right ... all except you.

CANTWELL. *(Smiles at Russell.)* And why wasn't I?

MARCUS. I ... well ... I don't know. I suppose it's in the records or something. But I know I thought then what a lot of people thought: how Joe must've pulled some pretty fancy wires to save his neck. Yes, sir, he was a real operator, he could get out of *anything,* and that's the truth ... Anyways, it's all there in the court martial; how he was one of them, named under oath by Lieutenant Fenn.

RUSSELL. *(To Marcus.)* Where is Lieutenant Fenn now?

CANTWELL. He's dead.

MARCUS. That's right, he died after the war in that plane crash, you remember the one? Out in Detroit, that freak one where the lightning hit the engine and ...

RUSSELL. *(To Cantwell.)* If you were innocent, why did Fenn name you?

CANTWELL. *(Coldly, carefully.)* Because I was the one who turned him in.

MARCUS. *(Stunned.)* You were!

69

CANTWELL. This clown wouldn't know but I'm ashamed of *you,* Bill, for not doing your homework, for not checking with a certain Colonel, now Major General, Conyers who was the Advocate General up there. *(Turns on Marcus, who retreats before him.)* You see, Shelly, when I found out what was going on I went to Conyers and told him what I had discovered about my roommate. We laid a trap for Fenn and he fell into it. At the trial I gave secret evidence against him and that's why he named me: *in revenge,* and that's why no action was ever or could ever be taken against me. *(To Russell.)* I even got promoted on the strength of having helped clear those types out of our command.

MARCUS. Oh, I bet that isn't so … I bet you'll find he sneaked out of it like he did everything else … I know Joe Cantwell …

RUSSELL. *(To Cantwell.)* Can you prove this? *(Cantwell nods. He crosses U. to desk.)*

CANTWELL. A few minutes ago I talked with the Advocate General. His name is Conyers. He's in Colorado now. He told me he would back me up. In every way. *(Cantwell gives Russell the telephone number.)* Here's his name and phone number. He's expecting a call from you, Bill. *(Like a carnivore, Cantwell stalks the terrified Marcus to the door.)* And now, Shelly Marcus, if you ever say one word about this to anybody, I will have you up for libel, *criminal* libel …

MARCUS. Now, look here, Joe, don't you threaten me … *(Marcus tries to get to the office door before Cantwell reaches him.)*

CANTWELL. In fact, I will involve you personally in that whole mess at Adak and by the time I finish with you …

MARCUS. Don't you bully me, Joe, don't you try to intimidate me …

CANTWELL. I'll make you wish you'd never been born! *(Just as Cantwell seems about to seize him, Marcus bolts into the connecting hall. He opens the corridor door. But to his horror, newsmen and photographers burst in. He is borne straight back to Cantwell, who smiles and straightens Marcus' jacket. Then he turns him about for the photographers, who want a picture.)* Just one second … *(Puts arm about Marcus' shoulders.)* Sure was swell to see you, Shelly. Next time when you drop by, bring the wife, bring … uh, Peggy. Mabel and I'd love to meet her. Love to see you both. You come see us now in

Washington. *(Poses again with Marcus.)* How's that?

PHOTOGRAPHER. Hold it! *(Marcus goes, surrounded by newsmen. Cantwell shuts the corridor door after them. He pauses a moment in the connecting hall, unobserved by Russell. Then he pulls himself together and returns to the living room.)*

CANTWELL. I'm sorry to disappoint you, Bill, but this won't work. I'm covered on every side. You won't be able to make this thing stick for two minutes. And I should also warn you: This is the kind of desperate last-minute smear that always backfires on the guy who makes it. Ask Art Hockstader. He'll tell you. *(Russell stares at him with a fascinated revulsion.)* Well, go on. If you don't believe me, you got General Conyers' number in your hand. Call him.

RUSSELL. True? False? We've both gone beyond the "truth" now. We're in dangerous country. *(Russell drops the paper with the telephone number on the sofa.)*

CANTWELL. *(Begins.)* Every word I said was true ...

RUSSELL. You are worse than a liar. You have no sense of right or wrong. Only what will work. *(Russell picks up the court-martial testimony.)* Well, *this* is going to work.

CANTWELL. But you're not going to use that now!

RUSSELL. Oh, yes! Yes! I'll use *anything* against you. I can't let you be president. *(Russell crosses to the bedroom. Cantwell follows. Russell starts to exit through the bathroom.)*

CANTWELL. Hey! What are you going to do? Bill, you're not really going to use that stuff. You can't. Look, it's ... it's too dirty! Honest to God, nobody will believe it! *(Russell pauses at the bathroom door. He looks at Cantwell; then he turns and goes into the bathroom. Cantwell, near breaking, shouts after him.)* OK Russell, go ahead, it's your funeral. Against me, you haven't got a chance. *(Cantwell paces back to the living room, not knowing what to do next. Then he picks up the telephone at the desk.)* Send Don Blades in ... and keep trying on that Colorado call. *(Cantwell crosses down C. Blades enters the living room from R.)*

BLADES. Well, what happened? *(Blades peers into the bedroom.)* Where's Russell? Joe? *(Sudden alarm.)* Hey, Joe! *(Cantwell is recalled from some private reverie. He looks at Blades; he smiles suddenly; his tone is casual.)*

CANTWELL. Oh, Don, hi.

BLADES. What's Russell up to? What's this all about? What's he got on you?

CANTWELL. *(Thoughtfully.)* You know what that guy said just now? He said I wasn't very sensitive about other people. He said I didn't understand character ...

BLADES. Is that what he came down here for? To give you a lecture?

CANTWELL. *(Nods.)* Yeah. Pretty much. *(Cantwell sees the paper with General Conyers' telephone number on it. He picks it up; he smiles.)* Well, I have news for him. I am a very good judge of character. *(Abruptly.)* You can release that stuff on Russell now. One copy to every delegate. *(Excitement.)* Don, we're home free. *(He rolls the paper into a tight wad.)* And I'll make you a bet: Russell quits before the first ballot. *(Cantwell flicks the wad across the room. The room goes dark.)*

## Scene 4

*The Russell suite. The next evening. The television set is on. Jensen watches it while going through papers at the desk. There is band music from the convention hall. In the bedroom, Alice finishes packing. The telephone rings.*

JENSEN. *(Answers it.)* Who? Oh, Senator Joseph. No, he's not back yet. No, I don't know what to do. He's still over at the hospital. He's with President Hockstader and there's no way to phone ... I guess we just stand by. How's the balloting? *(Frowns.)* Oh, no! *(Russell enters from the corridor carrying a newspaper under his arm, murmuring "No comment" to the press.)* Wait a minute, Senator. He's here. *(To Russell.)* Bill, it's Senator Joseph. He's in the convention hall. They're into the sixth ballot. It's still a deadlock. Cantwell's leading but nobody's got a majority. Merwin's sitting tight. Joseph says if you let him blast Cantwell now, we're in on the next ballot.

RUSSELL. What was the voting on the fifth ballot?

JENSEN. *(Looks at paper.)* Cantwell 474, Russell 386, Merwin 214 ... all the favorite sons are gone. And nobody's budging yet.

RUSSELL. What about Merwin? If I were to get his 214 votes ...

JENSEN. You'd win. But he's hanging on. Senator Joseph's trying to reach him now, to see if he'll take on second spot with you ...

RUSSELL. Cantwell must be trying the same thing ...

JENSEN. Merwin's holding out for the best possible terms.

RUSSELL. *(Smiles.)* He's showing unexpected character, isn't he?

JENSEN. *(Urgently.)* You've got to make up your mind! You've got to let our boys get that stuff on Cantwell to the delegates. We can ask for a recess before the seventh ballot. Then ...

RUSSELL. Tell the senator to wait.

JENSEN. But we *can't* wait.

RUSSELL. *(Firmly.)* I said, wait, Dick ...

JENSEN. *(Into telephone.)* Not yet ... *(He hangs up.)* Bill, what's wrong with you? We've lost a night and a day, but one word from you and we can still wreck Joe Cantwell.

RUSSELL. I know.

JENSEN. Then why are you holding back? What have you got to lose? Joe's done his worst. Every delegation's got a copy of your case history and believe it or not we're still in business. I don't know why, but we are.

RUSSELL. Which means perhaps that dirt does not always stick ...

JENSEN. Enough did. You lost three hundred votes because of it.

RUSSELL. But not all to Cantwell. Merwin picked up over a hundred of my votes. And that is a sign of something ...

JENSEN. Disgust.

RUSSELL. Or human decency.

JENSEN. Decency? At a *convention?*

RUSSELL. *(Smiles.)* I am an optimist. *(Russell goes into the bedroom.)*

ALICE. I packed. I thought no matter what happens, we'll be leaving Philadelphia.

RUSSELL. Yes, we'll be leaving.

ALICE. How was Art?

RUSSELL. They wouldn't let me see him today. He's still unconscious. *(Jensen, who has been watching the television set, leaps to his feet and goes to the bedroom.)*

73

JENSEN. *(Desperately.)* Bill, I don't want to press you, but will you please make up your mind. The sixth ballot's almost over and … *(Telephone in bedroom rings; Jensen answers it.)* Who? Oh it's you … He does? Now? *(To Russell.)* It's Don Blades. Cantwell wants to see you.

RUSSELL. I'm sure he does. *(Smiles.)* All right. Tell him to come up. I'd like to see Joe again.

JENSEN. *(Into telephone.)* OK. He'll see you. *(Puts receiver down.)*

ALICE. *(To Russell.)* What do you think Cantwell wants?

RUSSELL. A deal. What else does Joe Cantwell ever want. *(Picks up newspaper.)* Oh, have you seen his latest statement? "The rumors about William Russell's health have been maliciously exaggerated." He's wonderful!

JENSEN. Look, before he gets here, let me call Senator Joseph …

RUSSELL. No, Dick.

JENSEN. But yesterday you were willing to do anything!

RUSSELL. That was yesterday. I lost my temper. And did rather a poor imitation of Joe Cantwell. I was remarkably melodramatic. I even turned my own stomach. But today I'm myself again!

JENSEN. Bill …

ALICE. Leave him alone, Dick. *(Jensen crosses to the living room and turns up the TV.)*

RUSSELL. There is a certain relief to knowing that the worst has happened to you and you're still alive … and kicking. *(Hears the television set.)* Ah … there's my old friend Senator Carlin. True to the end. *(Russell goes into living room; Alice follows. Jensen turns up the volume.)*

CARLIN'S VOICE. *(Booming.)* This Sovereign State casts forty-four votes for the next Preznighstay's Joe Cantwell! *(Jensen turns the volume off.)*

RUSSELL. *(Thoughtfully.)* Senator Carlin has every characteristic of a dog, except loyalty. *(Blades and Cantwell enter. The press is violent in its attentions. With some difficulty, they are got out of the room.)*

BLADES. Gentlemen …

CANTWELL. Hello, Bill …

RUSSELL. *(Gaily.)* Hi, Joe! What a nice surprise, your coming here like this!

CANTWELL. Yes ... Mrs. Russell, I'm Joe Cantwell ... I don't think we've met. *(Cantwell shakes Alice's hand.)*

ALICE. How do you do.

CANTWELL. *(Mechanically.)* We talked on the phone, I guess.

RUSSELL. Sit down, Joe. *(Cantwell sits.)* I thought you would be busy working on your acceptance speech. Or is it already written?

CANTWELL. *(Begins.)* Now, Bill, as I see the picture.

RUSSELL. I've been working for months on *my* acceptance speech, trying to strike that delicate balance between humility and confidence.

CANTWELL. Yes. Now as I see this convention ...

RUSSELL. *You* of course have a gift for hitting the right note.

CANTWELL. Yes ...

RUSSELL. I like the way you always manage to state the obvious with a sense of real discovery.

CANTWELL. Yes. Now, Bill ...

RUSSELL. And that wonderful trick you have for ...

CANTWELL. *(Exploding.)* Bill, at least let me get one word in edgewise!

RUSSELL. *(Laughs.)* I'm sorry, Joe. I couldn't resist it. *(To the others.)* I was using Joe's technique: Never let the other man get started. Talk right through him. Also, whenever Joe starts a sentence with "Now, Bill ... " you know he's up to no good.

CANTWELL. *(Quickly.)* Now, Bill ...

RUSSELL. See? *(Cantwell controls himself with some difficulty.)*

CANTWELL. Very cute. Bill, this convention is really hung up and the way things are going we may never nominate anybody.

BLADES. And who wants to spend the next four years in Philadelphia?

CANTWELL. Believe me when I say I have given the whole thing a lot of thought: and I want you to be on my ticket.

RUSSELL. Well, that's very generous, Joe. But tell me, how can I possibly run for vice-president when I am at this very moment suffering from one of my frequent nervous breakdowns?

CANTWELL. There was no way of keeping a report like that secret. Anyway, you've got to admit we handled the whole thing damned well. I mean look at the papers: practically no mention ...

RUSSELL. Just as there was no mention of the fact that Art

Hockstader is dying?

CANTWELL. Art didn't want anybody to know how sick he was. Did he, Mrs. Russell? He was a great old guy. You know he's dead, don't you? *(Russell crosses D., shaken. Cantwell does not notice the other man's response.)* Now, as I see the picture, delegate-wise …

RUSSELL. I didn't know … Art was dead.

CANTWELL. Oh? Yeah, he died about half an hour ago. He knew it was all over last night when I saw him.

RUSSELL. *(Startled.)* You saw him?

CANTWELL. That's right. Just for a few minutes, while he was still conscious …

RUSSELL. Oh, no, no! Don't tell us that Art Hockstader with his dying breath said, "Bless you, Joe, go to it!" And handed on the torch. *(Cantwell gets to his feet, angrily.)*

CANTWELL. You certainly like to jump to conclusions, don't you? If you really want to know what Art said, I'll tell you: He said, "To hell with both of you," meaning you as well as me.

BLADES. He sure was a funny old bird. Full of piss and vinegar right to the end. But his day was done … just as well he conked out when he did. *(Alice goes into the bedroom.)*

RUSSELL. Will you two please get out?

JENSEN. Bill! *(Russell turns to follow Alice.)*

CANTWELL. Look, Russell, for a lot of reasons we want you on the ticket and, frankly, if I were you, I'd show a little … well, gratitude. *(Russell wheels about.)*

RUSSELL. *(Fiercely.)* Gratitude! Do you realize all I have to do is call Senator Joseph …

BLADES. *(Quickly.)* But you know that story about Joe was a bum rap, so how could you use it?

RUSSELL. Since when has the truth been a deterrent at this convention? It is also not true that I am mentally unstable …

BLADES. *(Quickly.)* But it *is* true that you had a mental breakdown, and that is a fact the voters should know. *(Cantwell stops Blades with a gesture.)*

CANTWELL. Bill, I solemnly promise before these witnesses that I will give you anything you want … the vice presidency, secretary of state … commitment or no commitment … it's yours if you throw me your votes on the next ballot.

76

JENSEN. *(Delighted.)* Bill, come on, they're scared!

BLADES. Oh, no, we're not!

JENSEN. They're sweating ice!

CANTWELL. I want a united front, for the sake of the Party.

JENSEN. Look at them squirm!

BLADES. Who's squirming? Anyway, we got all the votes we need right now.

JENSEN. Where?

BLADES. Governor Merwin.

JENSEN. He won't play with you.

BLADES. He's offered to. But Joe doesn't want Merwin on the ticket. He'd rather have the Secretary here ...

JENSEN. Merwin refused to be on the ticket with Joe and you know it. If he'd agreed, you wouldn't be up here, sweating!

BLADES. *(Angrily.)* I am not sweating!

JENSEN. Bill, we've got them. We've really got them. Let me call Senator Joseph?

CANTWELL. I wish you would. And tell him you'll support me, in the interest of Party unity, and that you'll accept the second spot on the ticket ...

JENSEN. *(Overlaps.)* And tell him you're ready to lower the boom on Cantwell? *(Russell at bedroom door. He looks at Alice. He decides.)*

RUSSELL. All right, call him. *(Alice returns to the living room.)*

JENSEN. Put me through to Senator Joseph. Extension twelve, convention hall ... Hello ... that you, Senator? Well, brace yourself. This is it. Our man is about to fight ... *(Russell comes to the telephone.)*

BLADES. *(Pleads.)* Russell, don't. You *can't* use that stuff. Joe's our only hope. He's the Party's only hope.

CANTWELL. Shut up, Don. We don't have to worry about Mr. Russell. He always does the right thing.

RUSSELL. *(To Cantwell.)* Thank you. *(Into telephone.)* Senator? This is William Russell. I'm coming down to the convention hall in a few minutes to make a statement. Before I do, I want you to get to the chairman of the next delegation pledged to me ... Utah? All right. Tell the chairman to announce to the convention that I have withdrawn from the race.

JENSEN. *(Aghast.)* Bill!

BLADES. *(Ecstatic.)* Mr. Secretary, I swear you won't regret …

RUSSELL. And that I am releasing my 384 delegates with instructions to support Governor John Merwin.

JENSEN. Merwin!

BLADES. But … but you can't … *(Russell puts the receiver down.)*

RUSSELL. But I can. And I have.

JENSEN. Merwin's nobody!

RUSSELL. Well, he is now somebody … *(Turns to Cantwell, who has sunk to a bench, his hand over his face.)* Neither the angel of darkness nor the angel of light … if I may exaggerate my goodness … has carried the day. We canceled each other out. *(Jensen indicates the television set.)*

JENSEN. *(Bitterly.)* Allowing the angel of grayness to win, as usual.

RUSSELL. The light blinds us … and we're all afraid of the dark. *(To Cantwell.)* I meant it, Joe, when I said I could never let you be president.

BLADES. *(Viciously.)* Well, you just cut your own throat. You are through in politics.

RUSSELL. Joe Cantwell is through in politics. *(Blades crosses to U. door.)*

BLADES. He had a deal! I bet he had a deal with Merwin all along, the tricky son of a … *(Blades slams the door after him. Cantwell looks at Russell for the first time; he is genuinely puzzled.)*

CANTWELL. *(Slowly.)* I don't understand you.

RUSSELL. I know you don't. Because you have no sense of responsibility toward anybody or anything and that is a tragedy in a man and it is a disaster in a president! You said you were religious. Well, I'm not. But I believe profoundly in *this* life and what we do to one another and how this monstrous "I," the self, must become "we" and draw the line at murder in the games we play with one another, and try to be good even when there is no one to force us to be good. *(Cantwell rises. He speaks carefully, without rancor.)*

CANTWELL. You don't understand me. You don't understand politics. You don't understand this country and the way it is and the way we are. You are a fool. *(Cantwell goes, shutting the corridor door after him. Russell shakes his head.)*

RUSSELL. We're not the way Joe thinks we are. At least not yet.

JENSEN. You don't even know Merwin. Nobody knows him. He's a man without a face.

RUSSELL. Don't underestimate him. Men without faces tend to get elected president, and power or responsibility or honor fill in the features, usually pretty well.

JENSEN. I'm afraid, Bill, your conscience is my enemy. *(Jensen goes offstage L. Russell looks after him a moment, then he notices the "Hustle with Russell" placard.)*

RUSSELL. *(Smiles.)* Well, everyone hustled except Russell. *(Notices television set.)* Here comes Utah. *(Russell turns up the volume.)*

DELEGATE'S VOICE. State of Utah at the instruction of that great American and Secretary of State William Russell *(Cheering.)* casts its fourteen pledged votes to the next Preznighstay's that great Governor John Merwin!

COMMENTATOR'S VOICE. This is the break in the deadlock! An unexpected development! There's real excitement down on the floor ... *(Russell turns off set.)*

RUSSELL. There it is! *(To Alice.)* Well, we've got work to do. Do you want to come down to the convention? Or wait here till I get back?

ALICE. I'll go with you.

RUSSELL. What ... do you think?

ALICE. I wish you'd been nominated.

RUSSELL. So do I.

ALICE. But I like the way you ... really won.

RUSSELL. Thank you. Life is choice, they say. I've made mine.

ALICE. *(Smiles.)* And without doing your one-two-three walk.

RUSSELL. You know, Alice, you don't have to stay with me, if you don't want to.

ALICE. I know I don't have to.

RUSSELL. *(Tentatively.)* But ... *would* you like to? Even though you'll never have the chance to be another Grace Coolidge?

ALICE. Now it's *my* turn to choose? *(Russell nods.)* Of course I'll stay.

RUSSELL. I'm glad. But I warn you: The fires of autumn burn notoriously low.

ALICE. *(Smiles.)* Well, I've been cold such a long time.

*(Russell takes her arm. They start to go upstage to the corridor door when reporters burst in. Ad-libbed cries of "Statement!" Flashbulbs go*

*off Russell finally quiets them.)*

RUSSELL. You may say that I think Governor Merwin will make a fine candidate, and I shall do everything I can to help him and the Party. *(Starts to go, pauses.)* Oh. *(Smiles.)* And I am of course happy: The best man won! *(Russell and Alice, followed by reporters, cross U., as the curtain falls.)*

## End of Play

# PROPERTY LIST

Phone
Drinks
Newspapers
Paper/documents
Luggage
Manila folder
Garment bag (ALICE)
Toothbrush (ALICE)
Shaving gear (RUSSELL)
Cigarette and lighter/matches (MABEL, MRS. GAMADGE)
Dresses (MABEL)
Watch (CANTWELL)
Electric razor (MABEL)
Pills (HOCKSTADER)
Dictionary (RUSSELL)
Photograph (MABEL)
Ashtray (RUSSELL)

# SOUND EFFECTS

Telephone
Door buzzer
Television
Band music

# NEW PLAYS

★ **MONTHS ON END by Craig Pospisil.** In comic scenes, one for each month of the year, we follow the intertwined worlds of a circle of friends and family whose lives are poised between happiness and heartbreak. "...a triumph...these twelve vignettes all form crucial pieces in the eternal puzzle known as human relationships, an area in which the playwright displays an assured knowledge that spans deep sorrow to unbounded happiness." *–Ann Arbor News.* "...rings with emotional truth, humor...[an] endearing contemplation on love...entertaining and satisfying." *–Oakland Press.* [5M, 5W] ISBN: 0-8222-1892-5

★ **GOOD THING by Jessica Goldberg.** Brings us into the households of John and Nancy Roy, forty-something high-school guidance counselors whose marriage has been increasingly on the rocks and Dean and Mary, recent graduates struggling to make their way in life. "...a blend of gritty social drama, poetic humor and unsubtle existential contemplation..." *–Variety.* [3M, 3W] ISBN: 0-8222-1869-0

★ **THE DEAD EYE BOY by Angus MacLachlan.** Having fallen in love at their Narcotics Anonymous meeting, Billy and Shirley-Diane are striving to overcome the past together. But their relationship is complicated by the presence of Sorin, Shirley-Diane's fourteen-year-old son, a damaged reminder of her dark past. "...a grim, insightful portrait of an unmoored family..." *–NY Times.* "MacLachlan's play isn't for the squeamish, but then, tragic stories delivered at such an unrelenting fever pitch rarely are." *–Variety.* [1M, 1W, 1 boy] ISBN: 0-8222-1844-5

★ **[SIC] by Melissa James Gibson.** In adjacent apartments three young, ambitious neighbors come together to discuss, flirt, argue, share their dreams and plan their futures with unequal degrees of deep hopefulness and abject despair. "A work...concerned with the sound and power of language..." *–NY Times.* "...a wonderfully original take on urban friendship and the comedy of manners—a *Design for Living* for our times..." *–NY Observer.* [3M, 2W] ISBN: 0-8222-1872-0

★ **LOOKING FOR NORMAL by Jane Anderson.** Roy and Irma's twenty-five-year marriage is thrown into turmoil when Roy confesses that he is actually a woman trapped in a man's body, forcing the couple to wrestle with the meaning of their marriage and the delicate dynamics of family. "Jane Anderson's bittersweet transgender domestic comedy-drama ...is thoughtful and touching and full of wit and wisdom. A real audience pleaser." *–Hollywood Reporter.* [5M, 4W] ISBN: 0-8222-1857-7

★ **ENDPAPERS by Thomas McCormack.** The regal Joshua Maynard, the old and ailing head of a mid-sized, family-owned book-publishing house in New York City, must name a successor. One faction in the house backs a smart, "pragmatic" manager, the other faction a smart, "sensitive" editor and both factions fear what the other's man could do to this house— and to them. "If Kaufman and Hart had undertaken a comedy about the publishing business, they might have written *Endpapers*...a breathlessly fast, funny, and thoughtful comedy ...keeps you amused, guessing, and often surprised...profound in its empathy for the paradoxes of human nature." *–NY Magazine.* [7M, 4W] ISBN: 0-8222-1908-5

★ **THE PAVILION by Craig Wright.** By turns poetic and comic, romantic and philosophical, this play asks old lovers to face the consequences of difficult choices made long ago. "The script's greatest strength lies in the genuineness of its feeling." *–Houston Chronicle.* "Wright's perceptive, gently witty writing makes this familiar situation fresh and thoroughly involving." *–Philadelphia Inquirer.* [2M, 1W (flexible casting)] ISBN: 0-8222-1898-4

**DRAMATISTS PLAY SERVICE, INC.**
**440 Park Avenue South, New York, NY 10016  212-683-8960  Fax 212-213-1539**
**postmaster@dramatists.com  www.dramatists.com**

# NEW PLAYS

★ **BE AGGRESSIVE by Annie Weisman.** Vista Del Sol is paradise, sandy beaches, avocado-lined streets. But for seventeen-year-old cheerleader Laura, everything changes when her mother is killed in a car crash, and she embarks on a journey to the Spirit Institute of the South where she can learn "cheer" with Bible belt intensity. "...filled with lingual gymnastics...stylized rapid-fire dialogue..." *–Variety.* "...a new, exciting, and unique voice in the American theatre..." *–BackStage West.* [1M, 4W, extras] ISBN: 0-8222-1894-1

★ **FOUR by Christopher Shinn.** Four people struggle desperately to connect in this quiet, sophisticated, moving drama. "...smart, broken-hearted...Mr. Shinn has a precocious and forgiving sense of how power shifts in the game of sexual pursuit...He promises to be a playwright to reckon with..." *–NY Times.* "A voice emerges from an American place. It's got humor, sadness and a fresh and touching rhythm that tell of the loneliness and secrets of life...[a] poetic, haunting play." *–NY Post.* [3M, 1W] ISBN: 0-8222-1850-X

★ **WONDER OF THE WORLD by David Lindsay-Abaire.** A madcap picaresque involving Niagara Falls, a lonely tour-boat captain, a pair of bickering private detectives and a husband's dirty little secret. "Exceedingly whimsical and playfully wicked. Winning and genial. A top-drawer production." *–NY Times.* "Full frontal lunacy is on display. A most assuredly fresh and hilarious tragicomedy of marital discord run amok...absolutely hysterical..." *–Variety.* [3M, 4W (doubling)] ISBN: 0-8222-1863-1

★ **QED by Peter Parnell.** Nobel Prize-winning physicist and all-around genius Richard Feynman holds forth with captivating wit and wisdom in this fascinating biographical play that originally starred Alan Alda. "QED is a seductive mix of science, human affections, moral courage, and comic eccentricity. It reflects on, among other things, death, the absence of God, travel to an unexplored country, the pleasures of drumming, and the need to know and understand." *–NY Magazine.* "Its rhythms correspond to the way that people—even geniuses—approach and avoid highly emotional issues, and it portrays Feynman with affection and awe." *–The New Yorker.* [1M, 1W] ISBN: 0-8222-1924-7

★ **UNWRAP YOUR CANDY by Doug Wright.** Alternately chilling and hilarious, this deliciously macabre collection of four bedtime tales for adults is guaranteed to keep you awake for nights on end. "Engaging and intellectually satisfying...a treat to watch." *–NY Times.* "Fiendishly clever. Mordantly funny and chilling. Doug Wright teases, freezes and zaps us." *–Village Voice.* "Four bite-size plays that bite back." *–Variety.* [flexible casting] ISBN: 0-8222-1871-2

★ **FURTHER THAN THE FURTHEST THING by Zinnie Harris.** On a remote island in the middle of the Atlantic secrets are buried. When the outside world comes calling, the islanders find their world blown apart from the inside as well as beyond. "Harris winningly produces an intimate and poetic, as well as political, family saga." *–Independent (London).* "Harris' enthralling adventure of a play marks a departure from stale, well-furrowed theatrical terrain." *–Evening Standard (London).* [3M, 2W] ISBN: 0-8222-1874-7

★ **THE DESIGNATED MOURNER by Wallace Shawn.** The story of three people living in a country where what sort of books people like to read and how they choose to amuse themselves becomes both firmly personal and unexpectedly entangled with questions of survival. "This is a playwright who does not just tell you what it is like to be arrested at night by goons or to fall morally apart and become an aimless yet weirdly contented ghost yourself. He has the originality to make you feel it." *–Times (London).* "A fascinating play with beautiful passages of writing..." *–Variety.* [2M, 1W] ISBN: 0-8222-1848-8

**DRAMATISTS PLAY SERVICE, INC.**
440 Park Avenue South, New York, NY 10016  212-683-8960  Fax 212-213-1539
postmaster@dramatists.com   www.dramatists.com

# NEW PLAYS

★ **SHEL'S SHORTS by Shel Silverstein.** Lauded poet, songwriter and author of children's books, the incomparable Shel Silverstein's short plays are deeply infused with the same wicked sense of humor that made him famous. "…[a] childlike honesty and twisted sense of humor." –*Boston Herald*. "…terse dialogue and an absurdity laced with a tang of dread give [*Shel's Shorts*] more than a trace of Samuel Beckett's comic existentialism." –*Boston Phoenix*. [flexible casting] ISBN: 0-8222-1897-6

★ **AN ADULT EVENING OF SHEL SILVERSTEIN by Shel Silverstein.** Welcome to the darkly comic world of Shel Silverstein, a world where nothing is as it seems and where the most innocent conversation can turn menacing in an instant. These ten imaginative plays vary widely in content, but the style is unmistakable. "…[*An Adult Evening*] shows off Silverstein's virtuosic gift for wordplay…[and] sends the audience out…with a clear appreciation of human nature as perverse and laughable." –*NY Times*. [flexible casting] ISBN: 0-8222-1873-9

★ **WHERE'S MY MONEY? by John Patrick Shanley.** A caustic and sardonic vivisection of the ░░░░░░░░░░░░░░░░░░░░░░░░░░░░░░░░░░░ razor-sharp wit. "…Shar░░░░░░░░░░░░░░ **IHUMW 812** ░░░░nanges is certainly potent.░░░░░░░░░░░░░░░░░░░░ **V648** ░░░░se wisdom." –*NY Times*. [░

★ **A F**░░░░░░░░░░░░░░░░░░░░░░░░░░░░░░░░░░░░░░░░ screwy comedy-drama t░░░░░░░░░░░░░░░░░░░░░░░░░░░░░░, surrounded by a cast of f░░░░░░░░░░░░░░░░░░░░░░░░an, the opera star Adelina ░░░░░░░░░░░░░░░░░░░░░░░░skyrocket to awe-some h░░░░░░░░░░░░░░░░░░░░░░nat you might call an ever░░░░░░░░░░░░░░░░░░░░*llage Voice*. [10M, 3W] IS░

★ **BRE**░░░░░░░░░░░░░░░░░░░░░░░░░░░░░░░░ the life of Prix, a Bronx r░░░░░░░░░░░░░░░░░░░░░r coming to matu-rity at t░░░░░░░░░░░░░░░░░░░░of a dramatic visit, where n░░░░░░░░░░░░░░░░░░░with humor, terse vernacular strength and gritty detail…" –*Variety*. [1M, 9W] ISBN: 0-8222-1849-6

★ **THE LATE HENRY MOSS by Sam Shepard.** Two antagonistic brothers, Ray and Earl, are brought together after their father, Henry Moss, is found dead in his seedy New Mexico home in this classic Shepard tale. "…His singular gift has been for building mysteries out of the ordinary ingredients of American family life…" –*NY Times*. "…rich moments …Shepard finds gold." –*LA Times*. [7M, 1W] ISBN: 0-8222-1858-5

★ **THE CARPETBAGGER'S CHILDREN by Horton Foote.** One family's history span-ning from the Civil War to WWII is recounted by three sisters in evocative, intertwining monologues. "…bittersweet music—[a] rhapsody of ambivalence…in its modest, garrulous way…theatrically daring." –*The New Yorker*. [3W] ISBN: 0-8222-1843-7

★ **THE NINA VARIATIONS by Steven Dietz.** In this funny, fierce and heartbreaking homage to *The Seagull*, Dietz puts Chekhov's star-crossed lovers in a room and doesn't let them out. "A perfect little jewel of a play…" –*Shepherdstown Chronicle*. "…a delightful rev-elation of a writer at play; and also an odd, haunting, moving theater piece of lingering beauty." –*Eastside Journal (Seattle)*. [1M, 1W (flexible casting)] ISBN: 0-8222-1891-7

**DRAMATISTS PLAY SERVICE, INC.**
440 Park Avenue South, New York, NY 10016  212-683-8960  Fax 212-213-1539
postmaster@dramatists.com  www.dramatists.com